STUDENT'S REVIEW MANUAL
to accompany
The American Nation
A History of the United States to 1877

STUDENT'S REVIEW MANUAL
to accompany

Garraty and McCaughey
The American Nation
A History of the United States to 1877

SIXTH EDITION

ELLEN HOWELL MYERS
San Antonio College

HARPER & ROW, PUBLISHERS, New York
Cambridge, Philadelphia, San Francisco, Washington,
London, Mexico City, São Paulo, Sydney

1817

Student's Review Manual to accompany Garraty and McCaughey:
THE AMERICAN NATION:
A History of the United States to 1877, Sixth Edition

Cover Art: "Off Mount Desert Island" by FitzHugh Lane.
Reprinted by permission of the Brooklyn Museum.

ISBN 0-06-042239-4

89 9 8 7 6 5

Contents

Introduction

The purpose of this Student's Review Manual is to help you study and review the textbook *The American Nation* (Sixth Edition) by John A. Garraty and Robert McCaughey. The Manual is not a replacement for or a condensed version of the text, but is instead a guide to its major points. The textbook is like a tree: The trunk contains important themes and generalizations, holding together and giving life to the branches of ideas, events, and personalities which have made history. The Student's Review Manual points out the major branches. These facts are useless unless they are attached to a major theme in a meaningful way.

Each chapter of the Review Manual is organized in the same manner. First there is a *Chronology,* which gives a few significant dates of events mentioned in the text. Then comes a *Chapter Checklist,* which summarizes the major points covered. This checklist is followed by a list of *Other Terms to Identify,* which points out less important but useful information to help you understand the material. The items are listed in the order in which they appear in the chapter. After *Other Terms* is a *Glossary* with definitions of words and terms that may not be familiar to you, listed alphabetically. Then there is a list of other words you should be able to define and a selection of *Sample Questions:* multiple choice and matching.

To use this Manual for best results:

First, read the assigned chapter in the textbook, keeping the Manual close at hand in order to look up unfamiliar terms or phrases in the *Glossary.* It is a good idea, too, to keep a dictionary nearby in case you need to be sure of the meaning of certain words, particularly those listed under *Words to Know.*

Then, to review the chapter, read the *Chapter Checklist.* You will find, along with the major points, other features such as small charts and *Presidents' Boxes,* the latter outlining important dates and events in the life of each president. *Other Terms to Identify* will help remind you of additional facts covered in the text.

After studying the textbook and the Student's Review Manual, spot-check your memory of the material by answering the *Sample Questions.* They will also give you practice in answering objective questions on quizzes and exams. If you find you cannot answer one or more of the questions, go back to the text and to the Manual for further study.

1 / EUROPE DISCOVERS AMERICA

CHRONOLOGY

1095–1290	Crusades to Holy Land
1492	Columbus landed in America
1500s	Protestant Reformation
1585, 1587	Roanoke Island settlements
1607	Jamestown, Virginia, founded
1620	Plymouth, Massachusetts, founded
1621	First Thanksgiving celebration
1624	New Netherland founded by the Dutch
1630	Massachusetts Bay colony founded by Puritans
1636	Rhode Island founded by Roger Williams
1664	New Netherland became New York
1681	Pennsylvania founded by William Penn

CHAPTER CHECKLIST

Spanish Beginnings in America

Christopher Columbus (1451–1506). The modern "discoverer" of America who, sailing under the flag of Castile, now part of Spain, made four voyages to the western hemisphere from 1492 to 1504 and died still believing that he had reached Asia.

Amerigo Vespucci (1454–1512). The Italian after whom America was named. His written account of voyages in 1499 and 1501 along the South American coast convinced Martin Waldseemüller, a German mapmaker, that Vespucci was the discoverer and that therefore the land should be named for him.

English Beginnings

Sir Humphrey Gilbert (1537?–1583). An Englishman who made two attempts (1578, 1583) to establish colonies in America. After the second attempt, in Newfoundland, Gilbert and the colonists decided to return home to England, and their ship sank in a storm off the Azores Islands.

Sir Walter Raleigh (1552?–1618). Half-brother of Gilbert who made several unsuccessful attempts (1585, 1587) to settle colonists on Roanoke Island, off the coast of North Carolina. Raleigh named the east coast of North America "Virginia" in honor of his unmarried queen, Elizabeth I.

Richard Hakluyt (1552?–1616). An English authority on the Americas who, in the late 16th century, stressed the need of the English crown to promote and financially support colonization in America. He stated the advantages in an essay, *Discourse on Western Planting.*

Virginia

1606, London Company. A joint-stock company composed of London merchants with royal permission to colonize what was then called southern Virginia.

1607, Jamestown. Colony founded by the London Company which became the first permanent English settlement in the New World. See the map on p. 20.

John Rolfe (1585–1622). His introduction of a milder strain of tobacco into Virginia provided a marketable cash crop and eventually made the colony economically successful. Rolfe also helped the colony by his marriage to Pocahontas, daughter of the Powhatan chief.

1619, House of Burgesses. A governmental body of delegates chosen in each district who met at Jamestown to advise the governor on local matters. It is considered the beginning of representative government in America.

Religious Division in England

Anglicans. Members of the official Church of England, which had been founded when Henry VIII broke with the Roman Catholic Church in the 1530s.

Puritans. Members of the Church of England who wanted to "purify" it by discarding those Roman Catholic practices that still remained.

Separatists. Members of the Church of England who thought it too corrupt and therefore separated from it. They formed denominations such as the Pilgrims and the Quakers.

Massachusetts

1620, Plymouth Plantation founded. About one-third of the colonists were Pilgrims, an English separatist group which had moved to Holland before sailing for the New World. They chose William Bradford as their first governor.

1620, Mayflower Compact. A document, signed on board the *Mayflower,* in which the passengers agreed to make laws and to abide by them.

November 1621, Thanksgiving feast. The Plymouth settlers celebrated a bountiful harvest with their Indian neighbors, thus establishing an American tradition.

1630, Massachusetts Bay Company. Composed of English Puritans, settled about 1,000 colonists in the Boston area.

John Winthrop (1588–1649). First governor of the Massachusetts Bay colony. See p. 90.

Freemen. Adult male settlers of the Massachusetts Bay colony who were permitted to participate in political affairs. Originally about 100 men were selected by the leaders of the colony, and thereafter only Puritan church members were included and allowed to vote.

General Court. The name used to refer to the colonial legislature of Massachusetts.

Connecticut

1636. Reverend Thomas Hooker and his Puritan congregation moved from Massachusetts and founded Hartford.

1639, Fundamental Orders. A governmental charter set up for the Connecticut River valley towns. It was patterned after the Massachusetts system, although males who were not church members could vote.

Rhode Island

1636, Roger Williams (1603–1683). He left Salem, Massachusetts, and founded Providence, Rhode Island, on land purchased from the Indians. His colony was the first to separate church and state.

Anne Hutchinson (1591-1643). A Boston resident who, like Williams, disagreed with the official Puritan theology and led some of her followers to settle in Rhode Island.

Maryland

1634. First settlers arrived in Maryland, a proprietary colony founded by Cecilius Calvert, whose title was Lord Baltimore.

1649, Toleration Act. A grant of freedom of religion to anyone who professed to believe in Jesus Christ. Lord Baltimore, a Catholic, had hoped that Maryland would be exclusively a Roman Catholic colony; therefore, when members of his own faith were quickly outnumbered by Protestants, he tried to protect them with this act.

Carolina

1670. First settlers arrived in Carolina, a proprietary colony named in honor of King Charles I of England.

Fundamental Constitutions. A plan of government which tried, unsuccessfully, to promote a feudal society in Carolina with landholding "land-graves" and "caciques" and peasants called "leet-men."

1712. The colony separated into North and South Carolina.

New York

1624. Dutch West India Company founded a colony known as New Netherland.

1664. England captured the colony. It was granted to the king's brother, James, Duke of York, who in 1685 became King James II.

New Jersey

1664. This proprietary colony attracted settlers by offering land on easy terms, freedom of religion, and a democratic system of local government. By the 1680s all the proprietors were Quakers, and members of that religious group settled there in large numbers.

Pennsylvania

1681. A proprietary grant was given to William Penn, a Quaker, who considered his colony a "Holy Experiment."

Quakers, or Society of Friends. A Christian religious group started in England by George Fox, who admonished his followers to "tremble at the name of the Lord," thus the name Quakers. They required no rituals or ministers, and their place of worship was called a meeting house, where the men sat on one side and the women on the other. They spoke one by one as the Inner Light, the illumination from God within each soul, spoke to them.

OTHER TERMS TO IDENTIFY

Leif Ericson. An explorer from Norway who, around the year 1000, was probably the first European to reach America. He touched the shores of Labrador in Canada.

Prince Henry the Navigator (1394–1460). A 15th-century Portuguese prince who from his court at Sagres encouraged the advance of navigational knowledge and the development of Portugal's trade with Atlantic islands and the African coast.

1494, Treaty of Tordesillas. A treaty signed at Tordesillas, Spain, by Spain and Portugal which moved the 1493 Papal Line of Demarcation to 370 leagues (1 league = 3 miles) west of the Cape Verde Islands. All non-Christian lands to the west of the line were reserved for Spanish commerce and colonization; those to the east of it were for Portugal. This treaty supposedly gave the New World, except for what became Brazil, to Spain, a claim which other European nations soon chose to ignore. See the map on p. 6.

Requerimiento. A document which Spanish conquerors read to American natives before attacking them. If the Indians did not recognize the authority of the Pope and the Spanish monarch, whose importance was duly explained in the Requirement, then the conquerors could consider the attack a "just war" and proceed.

Captain John Smith (1580–1631). An English soldier of fortune who spent two years in the early Jamestown colony. He encouraged the colonists to raise food and trade with the Indians rather than search for gold. He also explored, mapped, and named the New England area. Note the picture on p. 17.

Squanto. An Indian who was kidnapped and spent time in Europe, primarily in England, between 1615 and 1619. He befriended the Pilgrims at Plymouth, not only serving as their interpreter but also teaching them where to fish and what to plant. While acting as a guide for William Bradford, he got smallpox and died in 1622.

Proprietor. A man who was granted a large amount of land by the king; he in turn gave or sold his land to settlers, retaining political power over them. Eight of the thirteen original English colonies started as proprietary colonies.

Joint-stock company. A company formed by merchant capitalists who shared the expenses, and the losses, of a colonizing or trading expedition. The London Company, which founded Jamestown, is an example.

GLOSSARY

Antinomianism. A form of Christian belief that says faith alone is necessary to salvation. Anne Hutchinson, a Massachusetts Puritan, was persecuted for preaching her own variety of antinomianism.

commonwealth. The official title of some U.S. states, including Virginia, Maryland, Massachusetts, and Pennsylvania. For example, officially one says the Commonwealth of Massachusetts, rather than the state of Massachusetts. The term is used to mean a nation or state governed by the people.

Crusades. Christian military expeditions from 1095 to about 1290 to recover the Holy Land, present-day Israel, from the Moslems. These travels furthered European interest in oriental products.

dissenter. One who refuses to accept the doctrines of the established or national church. For example, the Quakers were dissenters from the Church of England.

Indies. A vague term used on early maps to describe Asia and nearby islands. These islands today are called the East Indies. Columbus thought he had reached the Indies and thus called the natives Indians.

Inquisition. A special Roman Catholic Church proceeding designed to discover and suppress heresy; in Spain, it was controlled by the monarchs who introduced the Inquisition in the colonies in 1569. Natives were exempted from its control on the ground that they were incapable of rational judgment.

Flanders. A region along the North Sea in what is today Belgium and France. Flemish merchants became wealthy making and selling woolen cloth.

Low Countries. A term for the region of Europe which today includes the Netherlands, Belgium, and Luxembourg.

Marco Polo (1254?–1324?). A Venetian who journeyed overland to China and later dictated an account of his adventures in the service of Kublai Khan. This book became the chief western source of information about the East.

New England. The northeastern region of present-day United States was christened "New England" by Captain John Smith after an expedition to the area of Maine in 1614. Today the New England states include Maine, New Hampshire, Vermont, Massachusetts, Rhode Island, and Connecticut.

patroon. An individual receiving a large land grant from the Dutch government. He had to settle at least 50 people on this grant, after which it became a hereditary fief. Patroons were granted land in New Netherland, present-day New York.

Pennsylvania "Dutch." German (*Deutsch*) settlers in Pennsylvania, attracted by William Penn's glowing descriptions of his colony.

Protestant. In the 16th century, one who protested the practices of the Roman Catholic Church. Today the term refers to a non-Roman Catholic Christian, such as a Lutheran, an Anglican, or a Presbyterian.

Protestant Reformation. The effort in the 16th century to revise the teachings of Christianity in western Europe, which resulted in the creation of Protestant churches separate from the Roman Catholic Church.

West Indies. The chain of islands which separates the Caribbean Sea from the Atlantic Ocean. These islands became colonies of the major European powers in the 16th to the 18th centuries.

WORDS TO KNOW

Define the following, using the dictionary if necessary.

acrimonious   libertarianism
altruism   pejorative
county palatine   proselytizer
heresy   serf

SAMPLE QUESTIONS

Matching

1. _____ A Portuguese who attempted to improve navigational knowledge, promote trade, and spread Christianity along the African coast.

2. _____ A Genoese navigator who sailed for Spain and tried to reach the Indies by sailing west.

3. _____ An Englishman who circumnavigated the globe, 1577–1580, and attacked Spanish treasure ships.

4. _____ An Englishman who sent colonists to Roanoke Island, near North Carolina, and

a. Richard Hakluyt.
b. Thomas Hooker.
c. Anne Hutchinson.
d. Prince Henry the Navigator.
e. Captain Francis Drake.
f. Christopher Columbus.
g. Sir Walter Raleigh.
h. Lord Baltimore.
i. Roger Williams.
j. William Penn.

named the general area
Virginia.

5. ____ An Englishman whose
essay, *Discourse on
Western Planting,*
stressed the military
and economic
advantages of
colonizing North
America.

6. ____ A Puritan minister
who led a group of
settlers into the
Connecticut River
valley in the 1630s.

7. ____ A Puritan minister
who was banished
from Massachusetts
and founded
Providence, Rhode
Island.

8. ____ A Boston settler who
questioned the
authority of the
Puritan ministers and
the Bible and,
banished from
Massachusetts, moved
to Rhode Island.

9. ____ A proprietor who
wanted his colony to
be a haven for Roman
Catholics.

10. ____ A proprietor who
wanted his colony to
be a haven for
Quakers.

Multiple Choice

1. The prosperity of Jamestown was ensured by:
   a. the discovery of gold.
   b. the development of fur trading.
   c. financial support by the king.
   d. the cultivation of tobacco.
2. The chief difference between the "Puritans" and the "Separatists" was that:
   a. the Puritans sought to purify the Anglican Church; the Separatists thought it too corrupt to salvage.
   b. the Puritans thought the Anglican Church too "popish"; the Separatists thought it not "popish" enough.
   c. the Puritans favored the higher clergy; the Separatists opposed them.
   d. there was no real difference.
3. The House of Burgesses was to Virginia as the General Court was to:
   a. Rhode Island.
   b. Connecticut.
   c. Massachusetts.
   d. New York.
4. Which of the following did not originate as a company-owned colony?
   a. Massachusetts.
   b. New York.
   c. Virginia.
   d. Maryland.
5. Who of the following did not move from the Massachusetts Bay colony to settle in a new colony?
   a. John Winthrop.
   b. Thomas Hooker.
   c. Roger Williams.
   d. Anne Hutchinson.

ANSWERS
Matching: 1. d 2. f 3. e 4. g 5. a 6. b 7. i 8. c 9. h 10. j
Multiple Choice: d, a, c, d, a

THE THIRTEEN ORIGINAL COLONIES

Name	Founded by	When	Char-ter	Made Royal	1775 Status
1. Virginia	London Co.	1607	1606 1609 1612	1624	Royal
2. New Hampshire	John Mason and others	1622	1679	1680	Royal (absorbed by Mass., 1641–1679)
3. Massachusetts					
Plymouth	Separatists	1620	None	—	(Merged with Mass., 1691)
Maine	F. Gorges	1623	1639	—	(Bought by Mass., 1677)
Mass. Bay	Puritans	1630	1629	1691	Royal
4. Maryland	Lord Baltimore	1634	1632	—	Proprietary
5. Rhode Island	R. Williams	1636	1644 1663	—	Self-governing
6. Connecticut	Mass. emigrants	1636	1662	—	Self-governing
New Haven	Mass. emigrants	1638	None	—	(Merged with Conn., 1662)
7. N. Carolina	Virginians	1653	1663	1729	Royal (separated informally from S.C., 1691)
8. New York	Dutch	1624			
	Duke of York	1664	1664	1685	Royal
9. New Jersey	Berkeley and Carteret	1664	None	1702	Royal
10. S. Carolina	Eight nobles	1670	1663	1729	Royal (separated formally from N.C., 1712)
11. Pennsylvania	William Penn	1681	1681	—	Proprietary
12. Delaware	Swedes	1638	None	—	Proprietary (merged with Penn., 1682, same governor, but separate assembly, granted 1703)
13. Georgia	Oglethorpe and others	1733	1732	1752	Royal

2 / AMERICAN SOCIETY IN THE MAKING

CHRONOLOGY

1636	Harvard College founded
1662	Half-Way Covenant in Massachusetts
1676	Bacon's Rebellion in Virginia
1686–89	Dominion of New England
1692	Salem witch trials
1733	Georgia founded
1740s	Great Awakening
1763	Parson's Cause
1763	Paxton Boys' uprising in Pennsylvania
1771	Regulators' protest in North Carolina

CHAPTER CHECKLIST

English Rulers in the 1600s	
1603–1625	James I
1625–1649	Charles I
1649–1660	Protectorate under Oliver Cromwell and son
1660-1685	Charles II
1685–1688	James II
1689-1702	William III and Mary II (1689–1694)

Economy

Southern colonies. Included Maryland, Virginia, North Carolina, South Carolina, Georgia. The agricultural South concentrated on export crops, such as tobacco in Virginia and Maryland, and rice and indigo in South Carolina.

New England colonies. Included New Hampshire, Massachusetts, Connecticut, Rhode Island. Overseas trade with Europe, Africa, and the West Indies became the driving force. See the map entitled "Colonial Overseas Trade," p. 67. Cod fishing from Cape Cod to Newfoundland was also important.

Middle colonies. Included New York, Pennsylvania, New Jersey, Delaware. Farming for local consumption and for the export of wheat to the Caribbean sugar islands was important. Maritime commerce made the seaports of New York City and Philadelphia thrive.

Land and Labor

Headright system. Originally used in Virginia, this system of land distribution provided that any person who came could claim 50 acres of unoccupied land for himself and for every dependent and servant he brought to America. To "seat" a claim and receive title to the property, he must mark out its boundaries, plant a crop, and construct some sort of habitation. The headright system prevailed throughout the South, as well as in Pennsylvania and New Jersey.

Quitrent. A fixed annual payment or tax which provided a way for the proprietors to derive income from their colonies. It "quit" or freed the recipient of the headright from feudal obligations to his lord. Medieval in origin, the tax was unpopular and was effectively collected only in Maryland.

Indentured servant system. Immigrants to the colonies paid for their passage by selling their future labor for a period of about five years. The indentured servant signed on with a ship captain who in turn sold him to an American buyer who wanted his labor and the 50-acre headright. Note the document on p. 45.

Black slaves. Introduced in English America by a Dutch ship at Jamestown in 1619. The first slaves may eventually have been freed, just as indentured servants were, but by the mid-1600s, the institution of permanent slavery was firmly established. Relatively few blacks were imported until the late 1600s, however, even in the southern colonies. See the map on p. 46.

Squatters. Individuals who settled on unclaimed land on the frontier without paying for it. When someone else wanted to establish legal title to the area, they often cried for "squatters' rights," the privilege of buying the land at the price for which it would have sold originally, before they had made improvements on it.

Religion

Established church. A church officially recognized by the government, with its ministers supported by public funds.

Anglicans. Members of the Church of England, which was the established church in the southern colonies.

1763, Parson's Cause. A lawsuit involving the payment of the Anglican clergy in Virginia. Ministers were usually paid in tobacco vouchers, but in 1759, the House of Burgesses passed the Two-Penny Act, stating that "tobacco debts" would be paid at a rate of 2 pence a pound, around one-half the market value. Indignant clergy appealed to the Privy Council in London, which voided the law. When Reverend James Maury sued for his pay, the young attorney Patrick Henry attacked the clergy as money-grubbing "enemies of the community." The judge ruled in Maury's favor, although the jury awarded him only one penny in damages. The token award reflected the lack of respect for the Anglican clergy.

Puritans. A religious group, followers of the teachings of John Calvin, who wanted to purify the Church of England of its remaining Roman Catholic traditions. The predominant sect in New England was Puritan Congregationalist, so called because in church government the local congregation was autonomous. The Puritans believed in predestination, or that God foreordains, even before a person is born, whether he or she will go to heaven. The Puritans searched for a sign that they were among "the elect," and good behavior along with material wealth were considered indications. The Puritans also valued education, so that all would learn to read the Bible.

1662, Half-Way Covenant. A rule in Massachusetts which provided for limited—or half-way—membership in the Puritan church. It allowed grandchildren of full church members to be baptized, even though the children's parents were not full members of the church. The individuals who had been baptized but had not had a religious "experience" which qualified them for full church membership were called "half-way" members and, after 1664, although they could not take communion or have a voice in church decision making, they were allowed to vote in civil elections.

Great Awakening. A religious movement throughout the colonies of the 1740s which featured an emotional rather than an intellectual approach to religion.

George Whitefield (1715–1770). An Anglican minister from England who made several speaking tours in the colonies during the Great Awakening, preaching very dramatic sermons which were particularly well-received in the frontier regions and in the South.

Jonathan Edwards (1703–1758). A Puritan minister famous for his emotional and vivid descriptions of eternal damnation, particularly in a 1741 sermon entitled "Sinners in the Hands of an Angry God." He was pastor (1727–1749) of the Congregationalist church in

Northampton, Massachusetts, and, after being dismissed by a vote of the congregation, he became a missionary among the Indians.

Intellectual Climate

William Byrd II (1674–1744). A wealthy Virginia landowner who proved himself to be equally adept at a number of diverse occupations: he grew tobacco, prospected for ore, served in the House of Burgesses, and collected a large library with 3,600 titles.

Reverend Cotton Mather (1663–1728). A leading Puritan clergyman in Massachusetts who wrote over 450 books on religion and science. He was considered an expert on demonology and vigorously encouraged the Salem witch-hunt in 1692. Mather also helped introduce smallpox inoculation in America when an epidemic hit Boston in 1721.

Enlightenment. An 18th-century intellectual movement, primarily in Europe. Thinkers of the period emphasized the power of human reason to understand the universe and devoted much time to collecting data about the world around them. The era is also called the Age of Reason.

Benjamin Franklin (1706–1790). The printer, inventor, diplomat, and politician who started his career in Boston working for his brother James Franklin, editor of the *New England Courant.* He moved to Philadelphia where he published *Poor Richard's Almanack,* developed the lightning rod and bifocal glasses, and served in the Pennsylvania Assembly as well as representing it in London as colonial agent. He later helped draft the Declaration of Independence, negotiate the peace treaty ending the Revolution, and write the United States Constitution. See his picture on p. 65.

Colleges

A primary purpose of colonial colleges was to train ministers. Greek, Latin, Hebrew, and Biblical studies were central to the curriculum.

1636, Harvard. The oldest college in English America, founded by the Puritans primarily as a training school for Congregational ministers. The college, located in Cambridge, Massachusetts, was named after John Harvard, who in 1638 bequeathed his library and half his estate to the new institution.

1693, William and Mary. A college in Williamsburg, Virginia, founded to give southerners an alternative to sending their children to

England for schooling. A shortage of faculty and funds kept it from offering much more than a grammar school education for decades.

1701, Yale. A college started by Puritan ministers and located in New Haven, Connecticut. The founders thought Harvard had become too liberal and wanted a return to more orthodox teaching and training of ministers.

Great Awakening colleges. In response to this religious revival, other educational institutions were founded.

1746, College of New Jersey (Princeton), founded by New Side Presbyterians.

1765, College of Rhode Island (Brown), founded by Baptists.

1766, Queen's College (Rutgers), founded by the Dutch Reformed Church in New Jersey.

1769, Dartmouth, founded by New Light Congregationalists in New Hampshire.

Conflicts Within the Colonies

1676, Bacon's Rebellion. A protest, led by the Virginia landowner Nathaniel Bacon, against the policies of Governor William Berkeley and his Green Spring faction which had ruled Virginia for over 30 years. Bacon and his frontiersmen, wanting a more aggressive policy against Indian attacks, marched to Jamestown to demand it. During the rebellion Bacon died, and later Berkeley executed 22 of the rebels.

1686–1689, Dominion of New England. The colonies of New Hampshire, Massachusetts, Connecticut, and Rhode Island were combined under one powerful governor, Edmund Andros. In 1688, New York and New Jersey were added. One of the purposes of centralizing the administration of the colonies was to enforce mercantilist regulations more effectively. After James II was deposed in England, the Andros regime, headquartered in Boston, was routed by a force of more than 1,000 armed colonists led by a contingent of ministers. Separate colonial charters were restored.

1689, Leisler's Rebellion. After the overthrow of Edmund Andros, Jacob Leisler, a disgruntled merchant and militia captain, seized control of the government of New York. After two years he was overthrown and sent to the gallows, that is, hanged. Yet for two decades his supporters and his opponents continued to struggle.

1763, Paxton Boys. Frontiersmen in Pennsylvania who protested eastern indifference to Indian attacks by raiding an Indian village and then marching on Philadelphia, where they were talked out of attacking the town by a delegation led by Benjamin Franklin.

1771, Regulators. A band of North Carolina frontiersmen who protested their lack of representation in the assembly. They were defeated in a pitched battle against 1,200 troops, and their leaders were executed. Like Bacon's Rebellion in Virginia and the Paxton Boys uprising in Pennsylvania, this protest indicated widespread discontent on the part of westerners toward eastern-dominated colonial governments.

OTHER TERMS TO IDENTIFY

James Oglethorpe (1696–1785). A British general and a member of the House of Commons for 32 years who, while chairing a committee on prison conditions, became interested in establishing a colony for those imprisoned for debt. He and other philanthropists secured a charter in 1732, and the next year the trustees founded Georgia.

Georgia. When Savannah was founded in 1733, land grants were limited to 50 acres, and slavery and alcohol were forbidden. Originally a proprietary colony under a group of "trustees," Georgia became a royal colony in 1752. By that time settlers had already found ways to get around the restrictions, and Georgia developed an economy much like South Carolina's.

Eliza Lucas (1722–1793). Married to Charles Pinckney and credited with introducing indigo, used for blue dye, to be grown as a cash crop in South Carolina.

1688, Glorious Revolution. James II, a Roman Catholic, was forced to vacate the throne of England and flee to France. His Protestant daughter, Mary, and her husband, William, were offered the throne, but only after they promised certain rights to Parliament. This bloodless "revolution" marked a turning point in Parliament's power versus that of the Crown.

John Peter Zenger (1697–1746). A printer who published the New York *Weekly Journal,* which opposed the policies of Governor William Cosby. Charged with seditious libel, that is, criticizing the government, he was tried in 1735. Zenger's attorney argued that the criticisms were true and therefore should be allowed to be printed. This reasoning, although contrary to English law at the time, persuaded the jury to acquit Zenger. This case was considered a landmark event in the development of freedom of the press.

GLOSSARY

ague. Chills accompanied by shaking. In Virginia most newcomers underwent "seasoning," a period of illness characterized by fever and ague.

Arminianism. The religious doctrines of Jacobus Arminius (1560–1609), a Dutch Protestant theologian who opposed John Calvin's doctrine of predestination. He placed more emphasis on free will and the importance of good works. Solomon Stoddard, minister of the Congregationalist church in Northampton, Massachusetts, embraced the easy ways of Arminianism, but these views were rejected by his grandson, Jonathan Edwards, who became pastor of the same church in 1727.

bounty. A government subsidy to promote production. Parliament placed a bounty on indigo grown in South Carolina because the blue dye was important in the British woolens industry.

factor. A business agent who acted as a middleman. For a fee, he arranged for the planters' export crops to be sold in England and then filled their orders for furniture or other manufactured items to be shipped to America. When the exchange was not equal, he arranged for credit for the planter.

infant damnation. The belief that unbaptized babies who died would go to hell, not because of their own sins, but because of the doctrine of original sin. At birth, one inherited the original sin first committed by Adam and Eve, who ate the forbidden fruit in the Garden of Eden; this sin could be washed away through baptism.

itinerant. One who travels from place to place, especially to preach. There were many itinerant ministers during the Great Awakening who went from place to place leading religious revivals.

orrery. A mechanical model representing the motions of the planets in the solar system. It derived its name from an Englishman, Charles Boyle (1676–1731), Earl of Orrery, for whom one was made. The first orrery made in America was completed in 1767 by David Rittenhouse. Note the picture on p. 77. This interest in the solar system was typical of the 18th century Enlightenment.

"peculiar institution." A term often used by southerners to refer to slavery.

pound. The basic monetary unit of Great Britain, symbol £. It dates back to the Roman occupation of England when £ was short for *Libra,* a unit of weight corresponding to the pound.

Scotch–Irish. Scots, living in Ireland, who moved on to America. In the early 1600s James I, to further the conquest of Catholic Ireland, had moved Presbyterian Scots to the northern Irish county of Ulster. But 100 years later, the descendants of these Scotch-Irish, or Scots living in northern Ireland, were persecuted. They were not allowed to export their woolens; they were forced to conform their religious practices to those of the Anglican Church; and as their long-term leases expired, they were forced to pay higher rent on their farmland. Instead of signing new leases, many Scotch-Irish moved to the American frontier where some of them fought the Indians just as they had fought the Irish.

tidewater. Water affected by the ebb and flow of the tide, that is, near the ocean. Note the area referred to as "tidewater" Virginia on the map, p. 42.

WORDS TO KNOW

Define the following, using a dictionary if necessary.

acculturation	pilferage
commutation	polygonal
demographic	pyrotechnics
heterogeneity	secularization

SAMPLE QUESTIONS

Matching

1. _____ Members of a religious denomination who were called Congregationalists.

2. _____ An 18th-century religious movement which advocated an emotional approach to religion.

3. _____ Farmers who settled on land without obtaining legal title to it.

4. _____ A general term for a church whose ministers were supported by public funds.

5. _____ A tax paid to the proprietor of a colony in recognition of his "sovereignty."

6. _____ A grant of unsettled land, usually 50 acres, to an immigrant, or to a person who paid the passage of an indentured servant.

7. _____ The term for the colonial legislature in Massachusetts.

8. _____ A European intellectual movement which emphasized human reasoning and

a. General Court.
b. squatters.
c. Paxton Boys.
d. Puritans.
e. Enlightenment.
f. Bacon's Rebellion.
g. established church.
h. Great Awakening.
i. quitrent.
j. headright.

man's ability to
understand the
universe.

9. _____ An uprising of Virginia
frontiersmen protesting
the colonial
government's Indian
policy.

10. _____ A group from western
Pennsylvania who
marched on
Philadelphia protesting
eastern indifference to
Indian attacks.

Multiple Choice

1. The terms tidewater, Eastern Shore, and back country refer to
geographic areas in the:
   a. New England colonies.
   b. Middle colonies.
   c. Southern colonies.
   d. British West Indies.
2. Under the indenture system, the servant was bound:
   a. for a year.
   b. for approximately five years.
   c. for life.
   d. until he could purchase his freedom.
3. Which of the following was not a minister of the Great Awakening?
   a. Jonathan Edwards.
   b. Increase Mather.
   c. George Whitefield.
   d. James Oglethorpe.
4. Which one of the following is incorrectly paired?
   a. Rutgers : Anglicans.
   b. Harvard : Puritans.
   c. Princeton : Presbyterians.
   d. Brown : Baptists.

5. Which one of the following pairs did not have the same occupation?
   a. John Peter Zenger and James Franklin.
   b. Cotton Mather and Jonathan Edwards.
   c. William Berkeley and William Phips.
   d. William Byrd and Edmund Andros.

ANSWERS
Matching: 1. d 2. h 3. b 4. g 5. i 6. j 7. a 8. e 9. f 10. c
Multiple Choice: c, b, d, a, d

3 / AMERICA IN THE BRITISH EMPIRE

CHAPTER CHECKLIST

Government and Trade

COMPARISON OF GOVERNMENTS

England	English Colonies	United States After 1789
King	Governor	President
Parliament		Congress
House of Lords	Governor's Council	Senate
House of Commons	Assembly	House of Representatives

Privy Council. A group of 15 to 20 of the British monarch's principal ministers who helped him watch over the entire administration of the kingdom, including colonial policy. They could disallow, or annul, colonial laws and served as the court of last appeal in colonial disputes. After the 17th century the Council declined in importance, and today it is simply an honorary group.

Board of Trade. Established in England in 1696, it nominated governors and other high officials for royal colonies and reviewed laws passed by colonial legislatures. The Board recommended to the Privy Council which laws should be disallowed. In order to influence the decisions of the Board of Trade, the colonies maintained agents, or lobbyists, in London; the most famous of these was Benjamin Franklin.

Mercantilism. An economic theory which states that a nation's wealth is based on the amount of gold and silver bullion in its treasury. There were several ways to achieve this wealth. One method was to own mines, such as those discovered by Spain in Mexico and South America. A second method was to acquire the bullion of other countries through trade. In order to do this, a country had to sell more to another country than it bought. This situation is referred to as "maintaining a favorable balance of trade." Note that a favorable balance meant that there was no balance; instead, a country wanted to export more than it imported.

Colonies were considered very important in the mercantilistic scheme because they could yield raw materials and also provide markets for manufactured products of the mother country. For example, England could buy lumber from the New England colonies rather than from a European country. Purchasing from a colony enabled England to keep her bullion within the empire, because the colony was considered simply an extension of the mother country.

Navigation Acts. A series of acts beginning in 1650 to regulate the commerce of the British Empire. Most important, all trade of the colonies had to be carried in English ships, which meant that all European products destined for America went to England first and were then reloaded.

Enumerated articles. As part of the Navigation Acts, certain products earmarked as articles which could only be traded within the British Empire. In 1660 they included sugar, tobacco, cotton, ginger, and dyes such as indigo (blue) and fustic (yellow). In the early 1700s rice, molasses, naval stores, furs, and copper were included.

"Salutary neglect." A term used by Sir Robert Walpole (1676–1745), a British politician, in referring to the fact that England often looked the other way when Americans violated the Navigation Acts. Walpole felt that the absence of overly strict enforcement was probably healthy, or "salutary."

1756–1763, Great War for the Empire

Called the Seven Years War in Europe. It was the fourth in a series of wars in which England opposed France.

Called the French and Indian War in America. English colonists fought the French and their Indian allies.

Campaigns took place in the Ohio Valley, where young George Washington made several unsuccessful expeditions to the area of Fort Duquesne, now Pittsburgh.

Another campaign area was Canada. Quebec fell to the British when the English General Wolfe defeated the French forces under General Montcalm. See the map on p. 99.

1763, Treaty of Paris. Great Britain acquired Canada and the eastern half of the Mississippi Valley, thus ending the French threat in North America.

In other treaties, Spain acquired New Orleans and the Louisiana Territory from France, and England temporarily acquired Florida.

England Tightens Controls

Proclamation of 1763. A declaration that no colonists were to cross the Appalachian Mountain range to settle. British officials hoped to check westward expansion and keep the colonies more closely tied to England; in addition, they hoped to pacify the Indians by helping them retain their lands. Note the map on p. 103.

1764, Sugar Act. Among the first acts passed by Parliament for the specific purpose of raising money in the colonies rather than simply regulating trade. The law placed tariffs, or import taxes, on sugar, coffee, wines, and other products. Taxes on European products imported by way of Great Britain were doubled, and the enumerated articles list was extended to include iron, raw silk, potash, and other items. Much emphasis was placed on enforcing the Sugar Act, and those accused of violating it were to be tried before British naval officers.

1764, Currency Act. Forbade the colonies to issue any more paper money. It was designed to prevent the colonists from paying creditors with depreciated money.

1765, Stamp Act. A tax on colonial newspapers, legal documents, licenses, and other printed matter. The colonists opposed it because it was a direct, internal tax, not a tax on trade within the Empire. The colonists protested in several ways:

Intercolonial Stamp Act Congress met in New York to protest taxation without representation.

An organization known as the Sons of Liberty staged demonstrations against the tax. Note the picture on p. 106.

Colonists not only refused to use the stamps, which would show that they had paid the tax, but also boycotted other British goods.

1766. Stamp Act repealed. On the same day, Parliament passed the **Declaratory Act,** which stated that the colonies were "subordinate" and that Parliament could enact any law it wished to govern them.

Differing Interpretations of Concepts

Representation

Virtual representation. The belief that every member of Parliament represented everyone in the British Empire, not just his own district. Even today an MP (Member of Parliament) does not have to live in the district from which he is elected.

Actual representation. The belief in America that members of the colonial assemblies represented the people of the geographical district in which they ran for office.

Constitution

To Englishmen, the constitution meant the sum total of laws, traditions, and judicial decisions which had developed over the centuries and which governed the country. The British constitution is considered flexible in that it can be changed by an act of Parliament or a judicial decision.

To Americans, a constitution meant a written charter, similar to those granted to the colonies. The present United States Constitution, adopted in 1789, is considered rigid, because it is above the ordinary laws of the land and can only be amended by a specially prescribed procedure, that is, a two-thirds vote in each house of Congress and ratification by three-fourths of the states.

Sovereignty

The English believed that ultimate political power, or sovereignty, could not be divided. After the Glorious Revolution of 1688, Parliament was considered sovereign.

Americans developed ideas about divisions of power, that is, that their own colonial assemblies, rather than Parliament, should have the final say concerning certain local matters.

Controls and Protests

1767, Townshend Acts. A series of levies or taxes on glass, lead, paints, paper, and tea imported into the colonies. The acts were named after Charles Townshend, who was chancellor of the exchequer, a position similar to today's secretary of the treasury in the United States. Colonists protested in various ways:

A boycott of British products was established.

A "Circular Letter" (1768) was sent out by the Massachusetts General Court, asking other colonies what action should be taken.

John Dickinson published *Letters from a Farmer in Pennsylvania to the Inhabitants of the British Colonies,* questioning the right of Parliament to tax the colonies.

1770. Townshend duties, except for a threepenny tax on tea, were repealed.

1770, Boston Massacre. Townspeople taunted British troops at the Custom House; when reinforcements were called in, they fired into the crowd, killing five Boston citizens. Propagandists called it a massacre and played up the event in the local press. See the engraving by Paul Revere on p. 111.

1772, *Gaspee* incident. The *Gaspee,* a British patrol boat, ran aground in Rhode Island while pursuing a suspected smuggler. Local people boarded the *Gaspee,* wounded the commander, and set fire to the ship. When the British tried to bring the culprits to justice, they could find no one to testify against them. This incident strengthened British conviction that the colonists were lawless.

1773, Boston Tea Party. The Tea Act of 1773 gave a monopoly on tea to the British East India Company, granting them the privilege of bypassing middlemen and selling tea directly to favored colonial merchants. The threepenny tax on tea from the Townshend duties remained. In Boston, local Sons of Liberty refused to let the tea be unloaded and taxed by thinly disguising themselves as Indians, boarding the ships, and dumping the tea chests into Boston harbor.

1774, Coercive Acts. Three acts applying to Massachusetts, passed by Parliament in retaliation for the Boston Tea Party.

Boston Port Act. Closed Boston harbor until citizens paid for tea.

Administration of Justice Act. Court cases could be transferred outside of Massachusetts if the governor felt an impartial trial was unlikely.

Massachusetts Government Act. Revised the colony's charter, giving more power to the royally appointed governor and making the governor's council appointive rather than elective, among other changes, weakening local authority.

1774, First Continental Congress. Met in Philadelphia with all colonies but Georgia sending delegates. It passed a resolution claiming for the colonial assemblies exclusive power of legislation, subject only to royal veto. The congress was an "extralegal," that is, unofficial, body which met to discuss common concerns.

"Continental Association." The delegates at the Continental Congress organized an "association" to boycott all British goods and to stop all exports to the empire. Local committees were appointed to enforce the boycott, by force if necessary.

OTHER TERMS TO IDENTIFY

William Pitt (1708–1778). British minister who recognized the potential value of North America and whose strategies contributed to English victory over France in the Seven Years War. See the map entitled "Pitt's Strategy, The French and Indian War, 1758–1760" on p. 99.

George Grenville (1712–1770). Prime Minister of England (1763–1765) who initiated a policy to get the colonies to help pay off the tremendous war debt which England had acquired during the Seven Years War.

John Locke (1632–1704). A British political philosopher whose *Two Treatises of Government* (1690) was influential in American thought before the independence movement. Locke stated that originally men had lived in a state of nature and enjoyed complete liberty but then had set up government to protect their "natural rights," particularly the ownership of private property. He further stated: "If any one shall claim a power to lay and levy taxes on the people by his own authority, and without such consent of the people, he thereby invades the fundamental law of property, and subverts the end of government." According to Locke, if a government exceeded its rightful powers, people could then cease to obey it and establish another government.

Samuel Adams (1722–1803). A Massachusetts patriot, second cousin of John Adams, who fanned the flames of the independence movement. He helped organize the Sons of Liberty and instigated the Boston Tea Party. In 1776 he signed the Declaration of Independence and later became governor of Massachusetts from 1793 to 1797. Note his portrait on p. 110.

1774, Intolerable Acts. A term used by the Americans to refer to the three Coercive Acts plus a new Quartering Act and the Quebec Act.

This legislation directly contributed to the outbreak of the revolutionary movement.

GLOSSARY

ad hoc. A Latin phrase meaning "for a specific purpose, case, or situation." The Privy Council formulated colonial policy on an ad hoc basis, treating each situation as it arose.

bullion. Gold or silver in the form of bars, ingots, or plates.

common law. The system of law used in England and countries colonized by England. Its distinctive feature is that it represents the law of the courts as expressed in judicial decisions. The grounds for deciding cases are found in precedents provided by past decisions. By contrast, the civil law system is based on *statutes,* that is, laws passed by a legislature. In reality a combination of both is used today because, with rapidly changing conditions, there is often no judicial precedent; therefore statutes have become more important.

El Dorado. A mythical place rich in precious metals and jewels, sought in Spanish America by 16th-century explorers. Originally the term meant "the gilded man" and referred to a tradition followed in Colombia by Indian chiefs who covered themselves with gold dust as an offering to the gods and then bathed in Lake Guatavita, washing the precious metal into the water.

French West Indies. The islands of Guadeloupe, Martinique, and what is today Haiti, in the Caribbean Sea.

nouveau riche. A French term meaning "new rich" or "one who has recently become wealthy." The term is often used critically to imply showiness or ostentation.

raw materials. Unprocessed natural products used in manufacturing. The English colonies provided such raw materials as lumber and naval stores.

WORDS TO KNOW

Define the following, using the dictionary if necessary.

accretion	fallacy
analogous	inexorably
aphorism	insatiable
burghers	recalcitrant

28

CHAPTER 3

SAMPLE QUESTIONS
Matching

1. _____ The group in England
which nominated
colonial governors and
reviewed the laws
passed in colonial
legislatures.

2. _____ An economic theory
which concentrated on
producing for export
and limiting imports.

3. _____ An act of Parliament
which stated all
colonial trade must be
carried in English
ships and that certain
items could only be
sold within the British
empire.

4. _____ A group of Virginia
land speculators who
opposed the French
presence in the Ohio
Valley in the 1750s.

5. _____ An agreement between
France and England in
which France
abandoned almost all
claim to North
American territory.

6. _____ A group in Boston
who resorted to
violence to protest the
Stamp Act.

7. _____ Accords reached by
American merchants
not to buy British
goods.

a. Ohio Company.
b. Sons of Liberty.
c. Board of Trade.
d. Continental Association.
e. Declaratory Act.
f. Coercive Acts.
g. mercantilism.
h. Navigation Act of 1660.
i. Treaty of Paris, 1763.
j. Nonimportation agreements.

8. _____ An act which stated
        that Parliament could
        enact any law it
        wished to bind the
        colonies.

9. _____ A group organized by
        the First Continental
        Congress to boycott
        British goods and to
        stop all exports to the
        empire.

10. _____ Acts which closed the
         port of Boston and
         provided for the
         transfer of cases to
         courts outside
         Massachusetts.

Multiple Choice

1. By the end of the colonial period *most* of the British colonies in
   America were governed by:
   a. the elders of the established church.
   b. a governor, council, and assembly, all elected by the people.
   c. a governor and council appointed by the king, and an assembly
      elected by the voters.
   d. the appointed representatives of the companies which had es-
      tablished the colonies.
2. The Proclamation of 1763:
   a. called for colonial enlistments to put down the Pontiac Rebel-
      lion.
   b. prohibited settlers from crossing the Appalachians.
   c. granted an extensive tract to the Ohio Company.
   d. prohibited colonial paper money.
3. England felt that Americans had parliamentary representation because:
   a. Americans had delegates in the House of Commons.
   b. the colonies had their own assemblies.
   c. the members of the House of Commons represented all citizens.
   d. the colonies were represented in the Continental Congress.

4. After the Boston Tea Party of 1773, the British:
   a. closed the port of Boston.
   b. repealed the tax on tea.
   c. banned the importation of coffee.
   d. summoned the First Continental Congress into session.

5. The First Continental Congress met to:
   a. declare war on England.
   b. protest the Coercive Acts.
   c. adopt the Declaration of Independence.
   d. protest the Stamp Act.

ANSWERS
Matching: 1. c 2. g 3. h 4. a 5. i 6. b 7. j 8. e 9. d 10. f
Multiple Choice: c, b, c, a, b

4 / THE AMERICAN REVOLUTION

CHRONOLOGY

1775	Battles at Lexington and Concord
1776	Declaration of Independence
1777	Battle of Saratoga
1778–1800	Alliance with France
1781	Battle of Yorktown
1783	Peace of Paris
1785	Land Ordinance
1787	Northwest Ordinance

CHAPTER CHECKLIST

Steps Toward a Final Break

April 19, 1775, Lexington and Concord. Towns in Massachusetts where the first real skirmishes of the Revolutionary War took place. General Thomas Gage, commander in chief of British forces in North America and also governor of Massachusetts, ordered troops to Concord to destroy a stockpile of arms which the Patriots had been accumulating. Paul Revere and others spread the warning, and when the Redcoats passed through Lexington on the way to Concord, they found about 70 Minute Men occupying the common. Gunfire was exchanged and eight were killed. The British returned to Boston and were harassed by sniper fire all along the road. April 19th is considered the first day of the Revolutionary War. Note the picture on p. 120.

May 10, 1775, Second Continental Congress. Convened in Philadelphia. John Hancock, a Boston merchant, was elected president of the

Congress, which included delegates from all the colonies. Some had attended the First Continental Congress as well. The Congress appointed George Washington of Virginia as commander in chief of the Continental Army and then turned to the task of recruiting men and obtaining supplies. See the portrait of Washington on p. 143.

June 1775, Battle of Bunker Hill. Fought on nearby Breed's Hill in Charlestown, Massachusetts, near Boston. General Gage's troops succeeded in pushing the Patriots from the area but paid a terrible toll, losing 1,000 men compared to the Patriots' 400. The battle is significant because after so much bloodshed the prospect of a negotiated settlement was greatly reduced.

January 1776, *Common Sense*. An essay by Thomas Paine which was very effective in swaying public opinion toward a complete break with England. Paine attacked the whole concept of an hereditary monarchy as being a corrupt institution and called King George III a "Royal Brute."

July 4, 1776, Declaration of Independence. Adopted by the Continental Congress. The document was primarily written by Thomas Jefferson, with additions by Benjamin Franklin and John Adams. The Declaration was in two parts. The first part tried to justify the Americans' right to revolt and was based on the ideas of John Locke. The second listed particular grievances against George III. Many Americans had blamed Parliament for the colonies' problems but had remained loyal to the Crown. This section of the document tried to indict the King personally. Note the picture on p. 122.

Tory. An American who remained loyal to England during the Revolutionary War, also called Loyalist. Tories included Anglican clergymen, merchants with ties to England, and rural elements in New York and North Carolina who resented the leadership within their own colonies. Between 7.6 and 18 percent of the white population were Tories, and about 100,000 left the United States after the war to move to other British possessions. Tories got their name from the English political party which traditionally supported a strong monarchy rather than a strong parliament. The American Tories remained loyal to George III, King of England.

The Conduct of War and Peace

October 1777, Battle of Saratoga. A Patriot victory in New York in which General Burgoyne surrendered with 5,700 troops. Note the map "Saratoga and Philadelphia Campaigns, 1777" on p. 129. The significance of the victory is that it sufficiently impressed France so that she diplomatically recognized the United States and signed a formal treaty of alliance.

February 1778, Alliance with France. France recognized the United States as being independent and signed a military alliance and commercial treaty with the new nation. Shortly thereafter France declared war on England. The treaty establishing the alliance was drafted by the French foreign minister, the Compte de Vergennes, and by the American commissioners in Paris, Benjamin Franklin, Arthur Lee, and Silas Deane.

1777–1778, Valley Forge. An area in Pennsylvania where Washington's Continental Army spent a terrible winter. The troops suffered from lack of food, clothing, and military supplies, and a number of them went home or signed up with the British. Valley Forge was considered a low point in the war for the Americans. Note the graph, "Washington's Troop Strength," on p. 125.

1781, Battle of Yorktown. Washington's troops and a French fleet trapped General Cornwallis at Yorktown, Virginia, and forced him to surrender in October 1781. This victory ended the last major battle of the war. See the map "Yorktown and the War in the South" on p. 130.

1783, Peace of Paris

Negotiated primarily by Benjamin Franklin and John Jay.

England recognized the United States as an independent country.

Boundaries set at Great Lakes to the north, Mississippi River to the west, and northern border of Florida to the South.

United States sailors could fish off of Newfoundland and dry their catch on beaches of Labrador and Nova Scotia.

Congress would "recommend" that confiscated Tory property be returned and would prevent further seizures.

Congress agreed not to impede British creditors from collecting their debts.

1777–1789, Articles of Confederation. Were proposed in 1777, finally ratified by all the states in 1781, and in force until the Constitution went into effect in 1789. The Articles gave a legal basis to the powers the Continental Congress had already been exercising. The individual states were considered independent and sovereign, and each state had one vote in the Congress, although they could send more representatives. A unanimous vote was required to pass most legislation. Under the Articles, the Congress could support the Army, conduct foreign relations, borrow money from foreign powers, and ask the states to contribute money. But the Congress could not tax, regulate domestic or foreign commerce, or enforce its authority.

Western Land

1785, Land Ordinance. Provided for surveying the western territories so that they could be sold by the national government. The land was divided into six-mile-square townships and further subdivided into 36 sections of 640 acres each. The land was to be sold at auction at a minimum price of one dollar an acre, and the money went into the national treasury. The 16th section of each township was earmarked for maintaining a school.

1787, Northwest Ordinance. Established a plan for setting up governments in the western territories so that they could eventually join the Union on an equal footing with the original 13. This ordinance specifically referred to the Northwest Territory, an area bounded by the Ohio River, the Mississippi River, and the Great Lakes, which was to be carved into three to five states. Note the map entitled "The United States Under the Articles of Confederation, 1787" on p. 141.

When the territory opened, a governor and three judges were appointed by Congress. After 5,000 adult males moved to the area, the people (adult males) could elect an assembly and send a nonvoting delegate to Congress, although the governor retained veto power over the assembly. When 60,000 persons moved into one of the political subdivisions, that area could draft a constitution, submit it to Congress for approval, and become a state. Its constitution had to provide for a republican, that is, an elected, representative government, and it had to prohibit slavery.

OTHER TERMS TO IDENTIFY

Minute Men. The local volunteer units in the Revolutionary War who were to be ready to protect their communities against the British at a moment's notice.

Paul Revere (1735–1818). A Boston silversmith who made a famous horseback ride on April 18, 1775, to warn Massachusetts villagers between Boston and Concord that the British troops were coming. In fact, Revere was captured in Lexington, and Dr. Samuel Prescott carried the message to Concord, but Revere's ride is well known because of a poem written in 1861 by Henry Wadsworth Longfellow entitled "Paul Revere's Ride."

Hessian soldiers. Professional soldiers, or mercenaries, hired by the British to fight in America. They were from the German province of Hesse.

John Dickinson (1732–1808). A Patriot who was considered a conservative leader because he favored reconciliation rather than revolt.

"Where shall we find another Britain?" he asked at the time of the Townshend Acts crisis. After hostilities broke out, he helped draft the Articles of Confederation and was later a delegate from Delaware to the 1787 Constitutional Convention.

Benedict Arnold (1741–1801). A Revolutionary general who participated in a number of successful campaigns against the British. But in 1780, as commander at West Point, New York, he plotted to turn that site over to the British in exchange for a sum of money and a commission in the British Army. The plot was discovered, and Arnold escaped before being captured. The following year he participated in several British raids against Americans and then went into exile in Canada and England.

Robert Morris (1734–1806). A Philadelphia merchant who was appointed by Congress to be superintendent of finances from 1781 to 1784. He reorganized part of the supply system for the army, set up a National Bank of North America and got the country back on a specie basis, that is, using coined money rather than the worthless paper notes which had led to the saying "not worth a Continental."

Society of the Cincinnati. An organization formed in 1783 by officers of the Continental Army just before they disbanded. George Washington was the society's first president, and membership was limited to the officers and their eldest male descendants. It was named after Cincinnatus, a Roman hero of the 400s B.C. who left his farm to become dictator and lead an army, and then gave up the reins of power after the crisis was over.

GLOSSARY

John Bull. A character often used in 18th- and 19th-century cartoons to represent England. Note the captions under the pictures on pp. 133, 218, and 350. He might be compared to today's Uncle Sam as a symbol of the United States.

livre. A unit of French money which is no longer used. It was originally worth one pound of silver.

minister plenipotentiary. A rank in the diplomatic corps. This title is used for one ranking between a minister and an ambassador. For example, in 1779 John Adams was appointed by the Continental Congress as minister plenipotentiary to conduct peace negotiations in Europe.

primogeniture. The right of the eldest son to inherit all of his father's estate, particularly if he died intestate, that is, having made no legal will. This medieval tradition prevailed in the South, the middle colonies with the exception of Pennsylvania, and Rhode Island; it was abolished during the American Revolution.

redoubt. A small, often temporary defense fortification. For example, the Patriots constructed a redoubt on Breed's Hill in 1775, which was overrun by the British.

"The Shot Heard Round the World." This phrase refers to the impact of the military skirmish at the North Bridge in Concord, Massachusetts, on April 19, 1775, beginning the American Revolution. The line is from a hymn by Ralph Waldo Emerson which was sung at the completion of the Concord Battle Monument, July 4, 1837.

> By the rude bridge that arched the flood,
> Their flag to April's breeze unfurled,
> Here once the embattled farmers stood,
> And fired the shot heard round the world.

town common. A tract of land belonging to or used by the community as a whole. It was frequently used in New England villages to pasture animals.

WORDS TO KNOW

Define the following, using the dictionary if necessary.

demagogue	geld
excoriations	ignominious
extralegal	paean
feinting	prorogue

SAMPLE QUESTIONS

Matching

1. _____ The Redcoats and the Minute Men exchanged fire on the common of this Massachusetts town, April 19, 1775.

2. _____ Redcoats and Patriots skirmished on April 19, 1775, at the North Bridge of this Massachusetts town which had been stockpiling arms.

3. _____ The Second Continental Congress

a. Philadelphia.
b. Ohio River.
c. Lexington.
d. Yorktown.
e. Bunker Hill.
f. Saratoga.
g. Concord.
h. West Point.
i. Mississippi River.
j. Valley Forge.

convened in this town in May 1775.

4. ____ This battle in 1775 was actually fought on Breed's Hill.

5. ____ The American victory at this site in 1777 made the French consider an alliance.

6. ____ Washington's troops spent a miserable winter here in 1777–1778.

7. ____ Benedict Arnold plotted to betray this fort to the British in 1780.

8. ____ The last major battle between the troops of Cornwallis and Washington took place at this site.

9. ____ As a result of the Treaty of Paris, 1783, this became the western boundary of the United States.

10. ____ This river was the southern boundary of the area governed by the Northwest Ordinance.

Multiple Choice

1. Samuel Adams, John Hancock, and Patrick Henry were all:
   a. Tories.
   b. governors appointed by King George III.
   c. participants in the Boston Tea Party.
   d. Patriots.
2. General Gage sent troops to Lexington and Concord because:
   a. he learned of the storage of a large amount of gunpowder there.
   b. he wished to provoke a colonial attack.
   c. the colonists were not paying the tax on tea.
   d. he wanted to stop Paul Revere.
3. The pamphlet written to demonstrate to the colonists the advantages of separation from England was called:
   a. *Exposition and Protest.*
   b. *New Freedom.*
   c. *The Federalist Papers.*
   d. *Common Sense.*
4. In the Peace of Paris (1783), the United States gained all of the following *except:*
   a. cancellation of American debts owed to British subjects.
   b. a western boundary at the Mississippi River.
   c. recognition of independence from Great Britain.
   d. fishing rights in the banks off Newfoundland.
5. How did England's administration of her colonies before the American Revolution *differ* from American administration of western territorial dependencies following the American Revolution?
   a. the authority of England as a central government was represented by a governor.
   b. the English colonies were subject to taxation by the mother country.
   c. England granted virtually no self-government to her colonies.
   d. England viewed the colonies as perpetual dependencies of the mother country.

ANSWERS
Matching: 1. c 2. g 3. a 4. e 5. f 6. j 7. h 8. d 9. i 10. b
Multiple Choice: d, a, d, a, d

5 / NATIONALISM TRIUMPHANT

CHAPTER CHECKLIST

Problems the Confederation Could Not Solve

Threat to the west posed by Britain and Spain

Britain would not surrender seven military posts in the Northwest, despite the Peace of Paris. Note the map "The United States, 1787–1802" on p. 167.

Spain periodically closed the lower Mississippi River to American commerce and denied the right to deposit goods at New Orleans while awaiting oceangoing vessels.

Disruption of foreign commerce resulting from independence

United States was now outside of the British empire and, under the rules of mercantilism, could no longer freely trade with her accustomed markets in England and British West Indies.

A tariff, or tax on imports, might have helped American "infant" industries, but Congress did not have the power to pass such laws, and an attempted amendment to the Articles could not muster the unanimous vote required.

Collapse of the financial structure

Wartime inflation followed by postwar deflation.

Stay laws. Laws which granted an extension to someone behind in paying off a debt. After the war many farmers pushed for the passage of "stay laws" to delay foreclosure on their farms. Foreclosure meant that their property was taken from them because of overdue debts or unpaid taxes.

1786–1787, Shays' Rebellion. A revolt led by the revolutionary veteran Daniel Shays in Massachusetts. He and other small property holders banded together to intimidate or close down courts to prevent foreclosure action against debtors. He and his group were finally routed when they tried to take supplies from a Springfield, Massachusetts arsenal, and Shays escaped to Vermont. He was later pardoned.

Steps Toward a New Constitution

1785, Mount Vernon Conference. Representatives of Virginia and Maryland met at Washington's Virginia estate, Mount Vernon, to discuss navigation on the Potomac River. They suggested a conference of all states to discuss common commercial problems.

1786, Annapolis Conference. Five states sent delegates to a conference at Annapolis, Maryland. One of the representatives, Alexander Hamilton of New York, suggested a meeting the following year in Philadelphia to propose changes to the Articles.

1787, Philadelphia Convention. All states except Rhode Island sent delegates to propose revisions of the Articles of Confederation, but instead they wrote an entirely new Constitution. Most of the delegates shared the following ideas.

Federal system. That political power be divided between the states and the national government.

Republican government. Ultimate authority resided in the people and not in a monarch.

Democracy. Government by the people, exercised either directly or through elected representatives.

Constitution

Great Compromise. A compromise between the large and small states concerning representation in the Congress. The large states had rallied behind the *Virginia Plan* whereas the smaller states supported the *New Jersey Plan.* The Great Compromise, sometimes called the Connecticut Compromise, provided for two houses in the Congress.

The House of Representatives was based on population and its members were elected directly by the people for two-year terms. The Senate gave equal representation to each state, and each state's two members would be elected for six-year terms by the state legislatures. The Seventeenth Amendment (1913) provided that senators be elected directly by the people rather than by the state legislatures.

Three-fifths Compromise. Three-fifths of the total number of slaves in a state would be counted, both in determining representation in the House of Representatives and in deciding each state's share of direct federal taxes.

Electoral College System. The indirect method used to elect the president. Each state could choose a certain number of electors, equal to the total number of senators and representatives from that state. The electors then voted for two persons for president. If no candidate got a majority, then the House of Representatives, each state casting one vote, could elect the president from the top five candidates. The runner-up became vice-president.

The system was slightly changed by the Twelfth Amendment in 1804. Since that time, the electors vote for only one candidate; if no one gets a majority, the president is selected from the top three by the members of the House. Balloting for vice-president is now done separately.

Judicial review. The practice of the courts of declaring a law void if it conflicts with the Constitution, although such authority is not specifically granted by the Constitution.

Checks and balances. Features in the Constitution designed to keep one area or branch of the government from becoming too powerful. For example, to become a law, a bill must get a majority vote in both houses of Congress and be signed by the president. But he can also veto it, and then it takes a two-thirds vote in each house to override the presidential veto. Another example involves the treaty-making power. The president or someone appointed by him can negotiate a treaty, but it must be ratified by a two-thirds vote of the Senate.

Ratification Controversy

Federalists. People who favored ratification of the new Constitution. Nine of the thirteen states had to approve the document before it went into effect, as it did in 1789. In general, the Federalists tended to be professionals or merchants. Many were wealthy, involved in commerce, and interested in an efficient government.

Antifederalists. People who opposed ratification of the Constitution. Many were small farmers, debtors, and people who were wary of the power granted to the central government by the Constitution. They were afraid it would destroy the independence of the states.

1787–1788, Federalist Papers. A series of 85 essays written primarily by Alexander Hamilton, with about 28 by James Madison and by John Jay. The essays appeared as a series in New York newspapers under the pen name of "Publius" and were designed to win support for adoption of the Constitution.

1788. Constitution ratified by the necessary nine states and legally in effect.

1789. George Washington elected president by the electoral college system and inaugurated in New York City, the first national capital. See the engraving on p. 161.

1791, Bill of Rights. The first 10 amendments of the Constitution. One of the criticisms of the Antifederalists had been that the Constitution made no provision for personal freedoms, and these amendments were designed in part to win their support. To amend the Constitution requires a two-thirds vote in each house and ratification by three-fourths of the states.

GEORGE WASHINGTON (1732–1799), 1st President

Born in Virginia and worked as a surveyor.
Participated in several campaigns against the French in the Ohio Valley.
Delegate to the First and Second Continental Congresses.
Commander in Chief of the American armies in the Revolution.
Lived at his estate in Virginia, called Mount Vernon.
President of the Philadelphia Convention which drafted the Constitution.
President (1789–1797).

Hamilton and the Treasury

Alexander Hamilton (1755–1804). Born in the British West Indies and, in 1773, emigrated to America, where he quickly became involved in the Revolutionary movement and served as Washington's aide-de-camp (1777–1781). He was a New York delegate to the Constitutional Convention and worked for its adoption by writing most of the *Federal-*

ist Papers. Hamilton was the first secretary of the treasury (1789–1795) and a leader in the Federalist party. He died in 1804 from wounds suffered in a duel with Aaron Burr. See Hamilton's picture on p. 163.

Funding of the national debt. The national government would recognize and pay in full all the "I.O.U.'s" which it had issued during the war to farmers, soldiers, and merchants in exchange for their produce and services, though many of these securities or notes were no longer in the hands of the original recipients.

For example, if a farmer had received a note for $100 during the war, he probably could not afford to wait to see if the government would eventually pay him. Instead, he sold it to a wealthy speculator for $75 in cash. When Hamilton decided to fund these securities or pay them off at par, that is, in full, these speculators received $100, although they had only paid $75 to the farmer.

Assumption of state debts. Since the war had been fought to benefit the whole country, the national government would assume, or take over, all the debts incurred by the individual states during that time. This idea was opposed by most southern states because they had already paid off their debts. However, a settlement was reached in the *Compromise of 1790* in which the state debts would be assumed, which would help the northern states; in return, the permanent location of the national capital would be in the south, on the Potomac River.

National Bank. Founded as a place where government income could be stored and from which government expenditures would be made. It also issued bank notes, which could serve as money. Hamilton's bank had a 20-year charter and lasted from 1791 to 1811.

The National Bank, or the Bank of the United States as it was called, should not be confused with present-day national banks. The latter are so called simply because they have a charter from the national government rather than from a state government. Today, we do not have one central bank; instead, there are twelve regional banks which were set up by the Federal Reserve Act of 1913.

Tariff. A tax on imported or foreign products. Some of the tariffs recommended by Hamilton were enacted in 1792. A tariff is designed to help local manufacturers by making the foreign product more expensive.

For example, the British made good-quality inexpensive woolen coats. Some Americans also went into this business, but with the price of constructing new factories and with high labor costs, they had to charge more than the British in order to make a profit. Consequently, the American consumer bought the cheaper British coat. But if a tax, or tariff, were added to the price of the British coat, it became more expensive, and Americans bought their own product. In general, the tariff helped the manufacturer but hurt the ordinary citizen, who had to pay the higher price.

Excise tax. An internal tax on a product designed to raise money for the government. Hamilton encouraged Congress to pass excise taxes, such as one on whiskey, in order to finance the funding of the national debt and the assumption of state debts.

Foreign Problems

FRANCE

1793, Citizen Genet affair. In 1793, a general European war broke out and President Washington issued a proclamation of neutrality. The French sent a special representative, Edmond Charles Genet, to seek support from Americans anyway by granting French military commissions and by licensing privateers to attack British shipping. Washington was annoyed at Genet's conduct and eventually asked that he be recalled to France. Meanwhile, however, his political associates had been overthrown in Paris, and rather than return to Europe, he sought political asylum and remained in the United States. He was referred to as "Citizen" Genet because in the French Revolution hereditary titles were abolished and people were simply referred to as "citizen," much as the Russians today might use the word "comrade."

ENGLAND

1795, Jay's Treaty. A treaty between the United States and England, signed in 1794 and ratified by the Senate in 1795. The American negotiator was John Jay, and the treaty was unpopular and loudly criticized by the new Democratic Republican party. Included in the treaty:

British evacuated posts along the Great Lakes. See map on p. 167.
American shipowners compensated for seizures in the West Indies.
American ships allowed to trade with British colonies in Asia.

But:

United States government must assure payment of pre-Revolutionary debts still owed British merchants.
"Rule of 1756" recognized by Americans. It was a British regulation stating that neutral countries could not trade in wartime with ports that were normally closed to them in time of peace. In other words, simply because the British were distracted by a war with France, American ships could not move in and try to trade with Barbados,

a British island in the Caribbean, which was closed to the United States, now that the United States was independent and no longer part of the British empire.

SPAIN

1795, Pinckney's Treaty. Negotiated by Thomas Pinckney to settle disputes between United States and Spain. The treaty gave America full navigation rights to the Mississippi River and the right to deposit goods at New Orleans before sending them on oceangoing ships.

The West

1794, Whiskey Rebellion. Farmers in western Pennsylvania protested the excise tax on whiskey by interfering with the courts and terrorizing law enforcement officers. President Washington considered their actions a threat to national authority and called up nearly 13,000 militiamen to break up the action. As a result of this show of force, the rebels ceased their activities, and the tax was collected peaceably.

1795, Treaty of Greenville. Indians abandoned claims to much of the Northwest Territory. It followed the 1794 victory of General Anthony Wayne at the Battle of Fallen Timbers and the British refusal to continue supporting the Indians in that area.

OTHER TERMS TO IDENTIFY

Adam Smith (1723–1790). A Scottish economist who published *The Wealth of Nations* in 1776. He opposed the closed trading systems advocated by mercantilism and favored free trade among nations. He opposed strict regulation of business by the government and instead supported nonintervention of government in the economic life of the country. His ideas greatly affected the United States' policies in the 19th and 20th centuries.

Charles Beard (1874–1948). An American historian who published *An Economic Interpretation of the Constitution* in 1913. His work suggested that the Founding Fathers at the Philadelphia Convention in 1787 were conservative, selfish businessmen trying to protect their own economic interests rather than concerning themselves with the needs of the majority. Much of Beard's controversial thesis has been discredited by more recent historians.

Loose interpretation vs. strict interpretation of the Constitution. The so-called elastic clause in the Constitution grants Congress the right to pass all laws which shall be "necessary and proper" to carry on its specified powers. Hamilton used the loose interpretation which stretched the powers of the national government. Jefferson favored a strict interpretation. For example, Jefferson opposed the creation of a national bank, claiming it was not "necessary" and was thus unconstitutional.

GLOSSARY

farthing. A British coin no longer used which was worth one-fourth of a penny. The word is still used to mean a very small amount. Immediately following the Revolution, the British would not have evacuated all western military posts, even if every farthing owed to British creditors had been paid.

guillotine. Machine designed to behead people by means of an ax or blade dropping down between two vertical posts. It was named after a French physician J. I. Guillotin, who proposed its use in 1789. This method of execution was commonly used during the French Revolution.

hard money. Gold and silver money as opposed to paper. Today the term often refers to any stable currency.

Hercules. A hero in Greek mythology who possessed tremendous strength. While he was still a baby, two serpents were put into his cradle and he strangled them. Alexander Hamilton referred to the United States as a "Hercules in the cradle."

legal tender. Acceptable money, currency that may legally be offered in payment of a debt and that a creditor must accept.

naval stores. A term originally applied to the timber, tar, and resin that were used to construct wooden ships and to make the seams watertight. Today it designates by-products of the pine tree, such as turpentine and pitch.

powdered lackey. A uniformed or costumed male servant wearing a powdered wig. Washington tried to set a tone of formality by having powdered lackeys at the entry of his presidential mansion in New York.

precedent. An act that may be used as an example in later similar cases. Washington, as the first president, was particularly concerned about establishing precedents.

staple product. A major item grown or produced in a region, such as tobacco in Virginia and fur in the Northwest Territory.

tonnage duty. A duty or charge per ton on cargo which is usually paid at a port or on a canal. For example, the 1789 Tariff Act placed heavy tonnage duties on foreign shipping to encourage Americans to use United States ships.

wampum. Small beads made from shells which were used by the Indians as currency.

WORDS TO KNOW

Define the following, using the dictionary if necessary.

adjudicate	entente
atypical	hamstrung
disparaged	intransigent
ebullient	voraciously

SAMPLE QUESTIONS

Matching

1. _____ An idea presented by Adam Smith in *The Wealth of Nations* which favored deregulation of commerce among countries.

2. _____ State legislation which gave debtors an extension of time before they had to pay a creditor.

3. _____ A process which resulted when Congress issued large amounts of paper money and the Continental dollar went down in value.

4. _____ Methods to control the three branches of the government so that no one of them gets too powerful.

5. _____ An agreement at the Constitutional Convention to base representation in the House on population and to have an equal number from each state in the Senate.

a. elastic clause.
b. free trade.
c. Bill of Rights.
d. tariff.
e. Rule of 1756.
f. checks and balances.
g. inflation.
h. strict interpretation.
i. Great Compromise.
j. stay laws.

6. _____ A portion of the
Constitution which
states that Congress
can pass "all laws
which shall be
necessary and proper"
to carry out its powers.

7. _____ The term commonly
used to describe the
first ten amendments
to the Constitution.

8. _____ A view of the
Constitution which
stresses *necessary* in
the "necessary and
proper" clause and
would limit the power
of the national
government.

9. _____ A tax on imports
designed to help
United States
manufacturers.

10. _____ A British regulation
stating that neutrals
could not trade in
wartime with ports
normally closed to
them in time of peace.

Multiple Choice

1. Delegates to the Annapolis Convention recommended the calling
of another convention to:
   a. strengthen the state governments.
   b. write a new plan of government.
   c. revise the Articles of Confederation.
   d. none of the above.

2. The group which was the most outspoken against the new constitution (1787) was called:
  a. Whig.
  b. Federalist.
  c. Antifederalist.
  d. Loyalist.
3. The first capital under the new Constitutional government was:
  a. Boston.
  b. Washington, D.C.
  c. Philadelphia.
  d. New York City.
4. A tariff was proposed by Hamilton soon after the establishment of the government, partly to:
  a. prevent the flow of valuable raw materials to England.
  b. encourage American shipping.
  c. protect the wages of American labor.
  d. encourage American manufacturing.
5. Jay's Treaty with Great Britain:
  a. abrogated the Rule of 1756.
  b. discontinued payment of prewar debts.
  c. secured evacuation of northwest posts.
  d. settled issues of neutral rights.

ANSWERS
Matching: 1. b 2. j 3. g 4. f 5. i 6. a 7. c 8. h 9. d 10. e
Multiple Choice: c, c, d, d, c.

6 / JEFFERSONIAN DEMOCRACY

CHAPTER CHECKLIST

Comparison of Hamilton and Jefferson

HAMILTON

Helped form the Federalist party.
Favored a strong central government.
Represented the business–commercial interests.
Favored England more than France.
Advocated governmental control by the upper classes.
Supported a national bank.
Favored the theory of loose construction of the Constitution by invoking the elastic, or "necessary and proper," clause.
Received support in urban areas of the northeast.

JEFFERSON

Helped found the Democratic Republican party.

Wanted a weak national government so as to conserve states' rights.

Represented the farming rather than the commercial interests.

Favored France more than England.

Felt government should be ruled by the informed masses.

Encouraged state banks and was originally opposed to the national bank.

Believed generally in a strict or literal interpretation of the Constitution.

Received support in the agricultural south and southwest.

Decline of the Federalists

1796, Washington's Farewell Address. Washington announced that he would not seek a third term, thus establishing a precedent which has only been broken by Franklin Roosevelt, who was elected four times. The speech is primarily remembered because he stated that Americans should avoid "permanent alliances," and later politicians used his argument to defend a policy of isolationism.

JOHN ADAMS (1735–1826), 2nd President

Born in Massachusetts; graduated from Harvard; and practiced law.

Delegate at the First and Second Continental Congresses.

Helped negotiate the 1783 Peace of Paris.

First United States minister to England.

Vice-president under Washington.

Member of the Federalist party.

President (1797–1801).

1797–1798, XYZ Affair. A diplomatic controversy between the United States and France. Adams tried to end French interference with American shipping by sending three commissioners to Paris: Charles Pinckney, John Marshall, and Elbridge Gerry. They discovered that Talleyrand, the French foreign minister, expected a bribe of $250,000 before he would begin negotiations. The agents who asked for the bribes became known as X, Y, and Z, and their demand was refused by the Americans.

1798, Alien and Sedition Acts. A series of acts designed in part to hurt the Jeffersonian Republicans.

Naturalization Act. A foreigner had to reside in the United States for 14 years rather than 5 years in order to be eligible for citizenship.

Alien Enemies Act. President could arrest or expel citizens of a country with which the United States was at war.

Alien Act. President could expel all aliens whom he considered dangerous.

Sedition Act. Made it illegal to write or publish "false, scandalous, and malicious" writings against the United States government. Under its terms, 25 Republican newspaper editors and publishers were arrested for criticizing John Adams and his policies, and 10 were convicted.

1798, Virginia and Kentucky Resolves. Passed by these two state legislatures in reaction to the Alien and Sedition Acts. The Virginia Resolves were written by James Madison and the Kentucky Resolves by Thomas Jefferson, and in theory they attempted to void the Alien and Sedition Acts within the borders of the two states. They presented the idea that a state, rather than the courts, could declare a law unconstitutional.

Convention of 1800. Abrogated, or officially abolished, the Franco-American treaties of 1778, under which the United States had supposedly been allied with France.

Election of 1800. According to the original Constitution each elector could vote for two men. The man with the majority of votes in the electoral college would win, and his runner-up would be vice-president. If no one got a majority, the election would be decided in the House of Representatives with each state getting one vote. In the 1800 election, the two Republicans, Thomas Jefferson and Aaron Burr, tied; the vote went to the House; and on the 36th ballot Jefferson became president by getting a majority of the states to vote for him. See the election graph entitled "The Revolution of 1800" on p. 180.

1804, Twelfth Amendment. Provided for separate balloting in the electoral college for president and vice-president, so that the runner-up would no longer be vice-president. This amendment was designed to prevent a recurrence of the problems in the 1800 election, which had occurred because of the development of two well-organized parties, a situation which the Founding Fathers had not foreseen.

Judiciary Act of 1801. Created six new circuit courts and 16 new federal judges. Adams filled these positions with conservative Federalists. The new appointees were called "midnight justices," since rumor was that Adams had stayed up until midnight before Jefferson's inauguration to sign their commissions.

THOMAS JEFFERSON (1743–1826), 3rd President

Born in Virginia; attended William and Mary; and practiced law.
Wrote the Declaration of Independence while a delegate to the
  Second Continental Congress.
Governor of Virginia.
Lived at Monticello, his estate in Virginia.
United States minister to France.
First secretary of state.
Founded the Democratic Republican party, along with James
  Madison.
Vice-president under John Adams.
President (1801–1809).
Founder of the University of Virginia.
Died on July 4, 1826, the fiftieth anniversary of the Declaration
  and the same day that John Adams died in Massachusetts.

Jefferson Met Challenges

JUDICIARY
  1803, *Marbury* v. *Madison*. The first Supreme Court decision which declared part of a law unconstitutional. Before President Adams left office, he had appointed William Marbury as a justice of the peace of the new District of Columbia. Although it had been signed, the commission had not been delivered, and Jefferson's secretary of state, James Madison, refused to do so. Marbury appealed to the Supreme Court to issue a writ of mandamus, that is, an order from the court requiring a public official to perform a specified duty, in this case to deliver the commission. Chief Justice John Marshall said Madison ought to deliver it, but the Court had no power to make him do so because that part of the Judiciary Act of 1789 which granted the Supreme Court the power to issue a writ of mandamus had been unconstitutional.
  Impeachment of judges. A majority vote in the House of Representatives is necessary to bring charges, or impeach, and a two-thirds vote of the members of the Senate present is required for conviction. Several Federalist judges were impeached. District Judge John Pickering was

convicted and removed from the bench; Associate Justice of the Supreme Court Samuel Chase was acquitted.

BARBARY STATES

1801–1805, War with Tripoli. For decades North African Arab states demanded "protection" money from European and American ships. Jefferson tried to curtail the practice, and Tripoli (present-day Libya) declared war on the United States. Jefferson did not achieve his goal, for tribute payments continued until 1815. But a more favorable treaty was negotiated.

LOUISIANA

1682–1763—France
1763–1800—Spain
1800–1803—France
1803–   United States

1682, LaSalle. French explorer who reached the mouth of the Mississippi River and claimed all the land drained by the river and its tributaries for France, naming it after King Louis XIV.

1763, Treaty of Paris. Ended the Seven Years War, and France gave Louisiana to Spain.

1800, Treaty of San Ildefonso. A secret treaty between Spain and France returning Louisiana to France, although the actual change did not take place until several years later. Napoleon wanted to grow food products in Louisiana to supply the French West Indian sugar islands, such as Saint Domingue.

1803, Louisiana Purchase. President Jefferson had sent James Monroe to join United States Senator Robert Livingston in Paris to attempt to purchase New Orleans and Florida. When Napoleon learned that he had lost the island of Saint Domingue, he authorized his Foreign Minister Talleyrand to sell all of Louisiana to the United States. Livingston and Monroe exceeded their instructions and purchased the area for about $15 million.

NEW ENGLAND FEDERALISTS

1804, Essex Junto. A group of New England Federalists organized to break away from the Union and establish a "Northern Confederacy." They tried to get the support of Aaron Burr, who was running for governor of New York. When Burr lost, the scheme collapsed.

THE WEST

1804-1806, Lewis and Clark expedition. Meriwether Lewis and William Clark led 48 men from St. Louis to the Pacific Ocean and back, gathering scientific data on plants, animals, and rocks, and establishing friendly relations with the Indians. Note the map "Exploring the Louisiana Purchase" on p. 190.

OTHER TERMS TO IDENTIFY

Democratic Republican party. Founded by James Madison and Thomas Jefferson in the mid-1790s. It was generally referred to as the Republican party. In the 1820s, Andrew Jackson changed the name of the party to Democratic. The Jeffersonian Republican party is today's Democratic party. The present Republican party started in the 1850s.

Citizen Pierre Adet. A French minister to the United States who tried to block ratification of the 1795 Jay Treaty with England and campaigned against the pro-British John Adams in the 1796 presidential elections.

John Marshall (1755-1835). A Virginian who became a leader in the Federalist party. During Adams' administration he served as minister to France, as a member of the House of Representatives, and as secretary of state. Adams appointed Marshall to the Supreme Court, where he served as chief justice from 1801 to 1835.

Aaron Burr (1756-1836). Republican politician from New York who tied with Jefferson in the Electoral College in 1800. The election was then decided by the House, and Burr, as runner-up, became vice president (1801-1805). In 1804 he ran for governor of New York and lost, partially because of statements made against him by Alexander Hamilton. Burr challenged Hamilton to a duel and killed him. See the picture on p. 188.

Pierre L'Enfant (1754-1825). Architect who submitted plans to Congress in 1791 for the capital city at Washington. He was dismissed the following year, and the plans were revised. But starting again in 1901 the capital was developed along the lines he had recommended.

Stephen Decatur (1779-1820). A naval officer who won fame in the war with Tripoli and later in the War of 1812 against England.

Napoleon Bonaparte (1769-1821). A military officer who became commander of the French Army in 1795, head of the government in 1799, and crowned himself emperor in 1804. After trying to conquer much of Europe and North Africa, he was finally defeated at the Battle of Waterloo in 1815.

Saint Domingue. Today the island of Hispaniola in the Caribbean is shared by two countries: the Spanish-speaking Dominican Republic, and Haiti, where a French-Spanish-African mixture called French creole is spoken. Formerly the whole island was called Saint Domingue (in French) or Santo Domingo (in Spanish).

1492. Columbus claimed Saint Domingue for Spain.

1697. France received western one-third of island.

1791. Racial unrest and revolt broke out on the French side led by Toussaint L'Ouverture, a former slave.

1795. Spain ceded her portion of the island to France but regained it in 1814.

1802. General Leclerc and French soldiers tried to recapture the island but failed, primarily because of yellow fever.

1804. The French colony became independent and was named Haiti.

1821. Santo Domingo, now the Dominican Republic, became independent from Spain.

Sacagawea. A Shoshoni squaw who, along with her French-Canadian husband, served as guide for the Lewis and Clark expedition.

Zebulon Pike (1779–1813). An army officer and explorer who made expeditions into the Louisiana territory and the Spanish southwest. He discovered the Colorado peak named for him. See the map "Exploring the Louisiana Purchase" on p. 190.

GLOSSARY

Continental Divide. A long stretch of high ground from each side of which the river systems of a continent flow in opposite directions. In North America the Continental Divide is formed by the crests of the Rocky Mountains.

Gallic. A term which means French, such as Gallic food. It is from the word Gaul, the ancient name for the territory which now includes France and Belgium.

junto. A small, usually secret, group that gathers for some common aim or purpose. The Essex Junto met to discuss secession of the New England states from the United States.

liberté, égalité, fraternité. A French phrase meaning "liberty, equality, brotherhood." It was used in France to describe the goals of the French Revolution and has since been used in other areas of the world to symbolize democratic movements.

pirogue. A canoe made from a hollowed tree trunk. Lewis and Clark used pirogues as they pushed up the Mississippi River in 1804. Today pirogues are still used in the bayous of Louisiana.

quasi-war. An undeclared conflict which resembles a war. The United States was involved in a quasi-war with France in the late 1790s.

Spartan. A person who resembles the Spartans in their indifference to physical discomforts, their austere manner of living, and their self-discipline. Sparta was an area in Greece where civilization flourished from the 7th to the 4th centuries B.C. Jefferson was considered somewhat of a Spartan in that he did not smoke, hunt, or gamble, and he partook sparingly of meat and alcohol.

WORDS TO KNOW

Define the following, using the dictionary if necessary.

anathemas	metaphysical
canard	mossback
dumbwaiter	pasha
juggernaut	pusillanimity
mantle	querulous

SAMPLE QUESTIONS

Matching

If the statement is true of Hamilton and his followers, place an H in the blank. If it is true of Jefferson and his followers, place a J in the blank.

1. _____ Believed that "Those who labor in the earth are the chosen people of God."
2. _____ Proposed the Bank of the United States and the Whiskey Tax.
3. _____ Wanted to commercialize and centralize the country.
4. _____ Favored the French Revolution.
5. _____ Admired English society and government.
6. _____ Feared the growth of cities and distrusted city workers.
7. _____ Pushed through Congress the Alien and Sedition Acts.
8. _____ Created the Democratic-Republican party.
9. _____ Argued that since the Constitution was a compact made by sovereign states, a state could declare a law of Congress unconstitutional.
10. _____ Favored cuts in military and naval expenditures to keep the budget in balance.

Multiple Choice

1. In his Farewell Address, George Washington:
   a. encouraged the growth of political parties.
   b. warned against forming permanent alliances.
   c. encouraged the country to seek better relations with England.
   d. abrogated the treaty with Spain.

2. According to the Virginia and Kentucky Resolves, where did the right to determine the constitutionality of an act of Congress finally reside?
   a. in Congress.
   b. in the states.
   c. in the president.
   d. in the Supreme Court.
3. In *Marbury* v. *Madison* Chief Justice Marshall established the power of the Supreme Court to:
   a. award damages to government officials who lost their jobs.
   b. issue writs which could order governmental officials to perform certain duties.
   c. invalidate federal laws held to be in conflict with the Constitution.
   d. remove governmental officials who refused to perform their duties.
4. Flags flew over Louisiana in which of the following chronological orders?
   a. France, Spain, United States.
   b. Spain, Mexico, France, United States.
   c. Spain, France, Spain, United States.
   d. France, Spain, France, United States.
5. In taking a position on the creation of the Bank of the United States, Thomas Jefferson expressed one point of view concerning his interpretation of the Constitution. In purchasing Louisiana, he took another. Which one of the following represents Jefferson's position in regard to the purchase of Louisiana?
   a. laissez faire.
   b. isolationism.
   c. strict constructionist.
   d. loose constructionist.

ANSWERS
Matching: 1. J 2. H 3. H 4. J 5. H 6. J 7. H 8. J 9. J 10. J
Multiple Choice: b, b, c, d, d

7 / AMERICA ESCAPES FROM EUROPE

CHAPTER CHECKLIST

Troublemakers for Jefferson

John Randolph of Roanoke (1773–1833). A member of the House of Representatives from Virginia for nearly 30 years. He generally took a strong states' rights position, and from 1804 he opposed Jefferson and his programs. Note the picture of Randolph on p. 204.

Yazoo land frauds. A land scandal in Georgia named for the Yazoo River running through part of the area in question. In 1795 the Georgia legislature sold territory in what is now Alabama and Mississippi to four land companies. When it was learned that the companies had bribed the legislators, the grant was rescinded, or canceled, even though some of the land had already been resold. Those who had bought land

59

from the companies denied Georgia's right to rescind the law and sought a remedy from Congress. Finally, Congress voted money to be granted to the victims of the Yazoo frauds. In 1810 the Supreme Court decision *Fletcher* v. *Peck* declared that Georgia's rescinding law had been unconstitutional.

1806–1807, Burr Conspiracy. Aaron Burr became involved in a western land scheme which led to his being tried for treason and acquitted. Whether he planned to detach part of western United States or conquer a section of the Spanish southwest is still unclear. However, his actions were betrayed by Louisiana territorial governor James Wilkinson, and Burr was brought to Virginia for trial. John Marshall presided at the trial, not as chief justice but as a member of the circuit court. Marshall encouraged a narrow definition of treason, and Burr was acquitted. See the sketch of Burr on p. 205.

Commercial Warfare with England and France

1799–1815, Napoleonic Wars. A series of wars in Europe with England and France on opposite sides. One method of fighting was to disrupt each other's economy through blocking trade. This tactic greatly affected Americans, who were trading with both sides.

1806, Berlin Decree. Issued by France, stating that all commerce with Great Britain was illegal.

1807, British Orders in Council. Instructions that ships could not go to ports on the European continent unless they first stopped at a British port and paid customs duties.

1807, Milan Decree. The French declared that any ship which stopped at a British port and paid duties would then be subject to seizure by the French.

Continental System. Napoleon's scheme of economic warfare against the British. He wanted to keep English ships out of ports on the European continent.

Impressment. The British practice of forcibly drafting Englishmen for service in the Royal Navy in emergencies. There were several methods of impressing sailors. One was to send "press gangs" into pubs in British ports. Another was to stop British merchant ships at sea and go aboard to impress sailors. A third was to stop neutral ships to look for British citizens. It was the third method which angered Americans because not only British but also Americans were impressed.

June 22, 1807, *Chesapeake-Leopard* incident. The British frigate *Leopard* signaled the unsuspecting American frigate *Chesapeake* off the

Virginia coast and sent a British officer on board to demand the return of four "deserters." When Captain James Barron refused, the British officer returned to his ship and the *Leopard* fired on the *Chesapeake,* killing three sailors. Captain Barron was forced to surrender, the alleged "deserters" were seized, and the *Chesapeake* was allowed to limp back to port. This action angered the American public and many wanted war.

December 1807–March 1909, Embargo Act. An act which forbade all exports from the United States. Jefferson hoped to prevent future *Chesapeake-Leopard* incidents, and he also hoped the boycott would put economic pressure on the European powers. The Embargo was unpopular among American merchants and was violated to some extent. However, it did mean a sharp decline in exports. Note the text chart "American Foreign Trade, 1790–1812" on p. 209.

1809, Nonintercourse Act. A United States law which forbade trade with Great Britain and France. If either country stopped violating American rights, the United States would resume trade with that country.

1810, Macon's Bill No. 2. A law named after Representative Nathaniel Macon of North Carolina which stated that the United States would resume trade with both France and Great Britain. But if either country stopped violating American rights, we would cease trade with the other. Soon after, Napoleon tricked Madison into believing that France would change her actions, so the United States stopped trading with Great Britain.

JAMES MADISON (1751–1836), 4th President

Born in Virginia and graduated from the College of New Jersey (Princeton).
Delegate at the Continental Congress.
A leader at the Constitutional Convention.
A founder of the Democratic Republican party.
Secretary of state under Jefferson.
President (1809–1817).

Other Problems Leading to War

Indians. They wanted to keep their lands.
Tecumseh (1768–1813). A Shawnee chief who bound together the tribes east of the Mississippi in a confederation. Its purpose was to

stop the advance of the white man into the Ohio Valley. During the War of 1812 Tecumseh fought alongside the British against the Americans and was killed in battle.

The Prophet. Tenskwatawa, the brother of Tecumseh, was known as the Prophet. He encouraged the Indians to give up white ways and to stop ceding land. See his picture on p. 212.

1811, Battle of Tippecanoe. Fought between Indians led by the Prophet and American troops led by General William Henry Harrison, governor of the Indiana Territory. The Indians attacked Harrison's camp, fell back, and then Harrison's troops destroyed Prophetstown, the village which the Indians had founded in 1808, where Tippecanoe Creek joins the Wabash River. The battle is significant because it shattered Tecumseh's Indian confederation, made Harrison a national hero, and convinced many western settlers, incorrectly, that the British had incited the Indians.

Depression and land hunger. The slow transportation and distribution system plus American commercial restrictions contributed to falling agricultural prices. At the same time, farmers wanted more land in the west.

War Hawks. The name given to young Democratic Republican congressmen who from 1810 to 1812 urged the United States to protect its national honor and fight the British. They were concerned about impressment and commercial warfare, but they also wanted to stop the Indian problems in the west and acquire Canada.

The War of 1812

1812–1814. Great Britain devoted little attention to the war in the United States. She was preoccupied in war with Napoleon's French troops, who were defeated at the 1815 Battle of Waterloo.

Naval Vessels.

Men-of-war. Wooden sailing vessels which included the ship of the line and the frigate.

Ship of the line. Large, square-rigged warship, carrying from 70 to 140 guns on two completely armed gun decks. The British had 7 ships of the line, the largest naval units in existence.

Frigate. A high-speed, medium-sized sailing vessel used from the 17th through the 19th centuries. At the beginning of the War of 1812, the Royal Navy had 34 frigates and the United States had 7.

Privateer. A privately owned ship authorized to attack enemy vessels during wartime. Several hundred American merchant ships lashed a few cannon to their decks and sailed off as privateers to attack British commerce, capturing more than 1,300 British vessels during the war.

1814, Burning of Washington, D.C. When defenses fell at nearby Bladensburg, President Madison and government officials fled the capital. British troops marched into the city and burned many of the public buildings, including the White House. This action marked a low point for the Americans in the war. See the map "The War of 1812" on p. 215.

1814, "The Star-Spangled Banner." After burning Washington, the British troops sailed toward Baltimore, Maryland, which was guarded by Fort McHenry. Francis Scott Key, a Maryland attorney, came on board one of the British ships to secure the release of an American prisoner. He was detained when the bombardment started, and through the night he watched to see if the American flag was still flying over Fort McHenry. The next morning he wrote the words to "The Star-Spangled Banner," which was later set to the tune of a popular English song "To Anacreon in Heaven." It was officially adopted as the national anthem in 1913.

1815, Treaty of Ghent. Signed in Ghent, Belgium, on December 24, 1814, and ratified by the Senate in 1815, this treaty ended the War of 1812. It was essentially an agreement to stop fighting since neither side made concessions. The British and the Americans agreed to restore all conquered territory and return to the *status quo ante bellum,* that is, to the way things were before the war.

1814–1815, Hartford Convention. A gathering of New England Federalists in Hartford, Connecticut, to protest the War of 1812 and to propose amendments to the Constitution. It was the New England commercial interests who were hardest hit by the wartime blockade. A few proposed separation from the Union. The convention proposed constitutional amendments which would require a two-thirds, rather than a majority, vote of Congress for the admission of new states and for declaring war. When news of the Treaty of Ghent arrived, their plans were ignored and their party discredited. The Hartford Convention is sometimes considered the "dying gasp" of the Federalist party.

1815, Battle of New Orleans. A great victory for the Americans, led by General Andrew Jackson, which took place after the treaty had been signed. After two weeks of probing the American line five miles below New Orleans, the British General Pakenham ordered an assault on January 8. When the bugles finally signaled retreat, the British had suffered 2,100 casualties, including nearly 300 killed. Thirteen Americans died, and fifty-eight more were wounded or missing. The battle strengthened American pride and nationalism and made Andrew Jackson a national hero. See the picture on p. 220.

Results of the War

Feelings of nationalism were increased. People felt pride in being Americans. European nations viewed the United States with new respect, realizing that our republican form of government was not going to be just a temporary experiment.

Indians were pushed farther west. As a result, new lands were opened to settlers.

Federalist party was destroyed. The party had experienced a brief revival led by a group known as the Young Federalists. But when the war which they opposed ended, their views found no support. The party ran its last presidential candidate, Rufus King, in the election of 1816.

Relations with England improved

1817, Rush-Bagot Agreement. Began the demilitarization of the United States-Canadian border. This agreement limited armed vessels for each power on the Great Lakes to one 100-ton vessel armed with an 18-pounder on Lake Champlain and another on Lake Ontario. An 18-pounder was a cannon, mounted on a ship, which fired cannon-balls weighing 18 pounds.

Convention of 1818. Allowed for the joint control of the Oregon territory for 10 years after which the agreement could be renewed. In addition, it set the 49th parallel as the northern boundary of the Louisiana Territory between the Lake of the Woods and the Rocky Mountains. Note the map entitled "The United States 1819" on p. 223.

Expanding United States' Role in the Continent

1819, Transcontinental Treaty. Negotiated by Secretary of State John Quincy Adams and Luis de Onís, the Spanish minister in Washington. It was ratified by the Senate in 1821. The United States acquired Florida in exchange for assuming $5 million in claims which the Spanish government owed American citizens. The treaty also established the Spanish boundary from Louisiana to the Pacific Ocean. Spain abandoned her claims to the territory north of California, and the United

States abandoned claims to Texas. See the map "The United States 1819" on p. 223.

FLORIDA

1513—Claimed by Ponce de Leon for Spain.

1763–1783—Owned by England, then returned to Spain.

1813—United States troops seized West Florida.

1818—General Jackson raided Seminole settlements in Florida.

1819—Adams-Onís Transcontinental Treaty signed.

1821—Senate ratified the treaty, and Florida became part of the United States.

1823, Monroe Doctrine. A statement of foreign policy which proclaimed that the United States would not meddle in European affairs and Europe should not interfere in the United States or in other countries in this hemisphere. These ideas, formulated by Secretary of State Adams and Monroe, were presented in President Monroe's annual message on December 2, 1823. The message was in response to two problems—Russian claims to the Northwest Coast and the independence of Latin America. It stated:

North and South America were no longer open to European colonization. This portion was to discourage the Russians along the Pacific coast.

The United States would not bother colonies which belonged to European powers, such as Canada, Puerto Rico, or Martinique.

Europe's political system was different from that developing in this hemisphere, and the two should not be mixed. The Latin American countries which had won their independence by 1821 had set up republics rather than monarchies, with the exception of Brazil, which had an emperor until 1889.

This policy statement was simply a speech, not international law, and had no real meaning until years later when the United States had the power to enforce it. It is still used today when the United States believes that a European country is interfering in the affairs of a country in this hemisphere. A recent example is the 1962 protest to Russia when she attempted to establish missile bases in Cuba.

OTHER TERMS TO IDENTIFY

Albert Gallatin (1761–1849). Secretary of the treasury under presidents Jefferson and Madison. Although he was a Jeffersonian Republican, his financial policies did not differ sharply from those of the original treasury secretary, Hamilton. Gallatin was a negotiator at the Treaty of Ghent and later United States minister to France and to Great Britain. He was also interested in Indian languages and customs and in 1842 founded the American Ethnological Society.

James Wilkinson (1757–1825). A professional soldier who at intervals in his career was suspected of accepting bribes. He was in the pay of the Spanish when, as governor of Louisiana territory in 1805–1806, he discussed with Aaron Burr various aspects of Burr's western schemes. Then Wilkinson betrayed Burr's activities to President Jefferson and was the prosecution's chief witness at the trial.

Rule of War of 1756. The British denied to neutrals the right to engage in trade during time of war from which they were banned by mercantilistic regulations in time of peace. For example, sugar from the French island of Martinique was to be carried to France in French ships. But during the Napoleonic Wars French ships were bottled up in port or distracted elsewhere, so United States ships tried to appropriate this trade. The British applied the Rule of 1756 and captured the American ships.

Reexport trade. As a way of getting around the Rule of 1756, Americans brought products from the West Indies to the United States first and then reshipped them to Europe, claiming that since the products had touched American soil, they were now American products.

GLOSSARY

Attila. A king of the Germanic tribe called the Huns from 434 to 453 A.D., he led a bloodthirsty invasion of Europe. Jefferson once referred to Napoleon Bonaparte as "the Attila of the age."

bayou. A marshy body of water which is a tributary to a lake or river. The term, based on an Indian word, was originally used by the French in Louisiana.

claims. Demands for payment made by the citizens of one country to the government of another. For example, if Indians from Spanish Florida raided Georgia and burned down a barn, then the owner might file a claim with the Spanish government demanding payment for the lost property. In the 1819 Transcontinental Treaty, the United States government assumed $5 million in claims which American citizens had been demanding from the Spanish government.

parapet. An earthen or stony embankment protecting soldiers from enemy fire. At the Battle of New Orleans, Jackson's troops erected an earthen parapet about 10 yards behind a dry creek bed, and there they made their stand against the British.

rapprochement. A reestablishment of cordial relations, as between two countries. After the War of 1812 an Anglo-American rapprochement emerged; that is, relations between the two countries improved.

state's evidence. Evidence voluntarily given by an accomplice who confesses the crime and testifies in court against previous associates. President Jefferson ordered blanket pardons to coconspirators of Aaron Burr who would agree to turn state's evidence.

tar. Informal noun for sailor. It is short for tarpaulin, a waterproof canvas used to cover and protect objects from moisture. Before the War of 1812, at least 10,000 British-born tars were serving on American ships.

treason. The offense of attempting by overt acts to overthrow the government of one's own country. Treason in the United States is defined in the Constitution (Article III, Section 3) as consisting "only in levying War against them, or in adhering to their Enemies, giving them Aid and Comfort. No Person shall be convicted of Treason unless on the Testimony of two Witnesses to the same Overt Act, or on Confession in open Court." Aaron Burr was tried for treason, but not convicted.

"twisting the British lion's tail." A term used in the 19th century referring to the Americans' practice of criticizing policies and making jokes at the expense of Great Britain. The lion is the symbol of England.

WORDS TO KNOW

Define the following, using the dictionary if necessary.

anomalous	macabre
epigram	parsimonious
immutable	pithy
largess	psychosomatic

SAMPLE QUESTIONS

Matching

1. _____ Republican congressman from Virginia who favored strong states' rights.

2. _____ Republican politician who planned to separate part of the West from the United States.

3. _____ The presiding judge at Burr's treason trial.

4. _____ The Shawnee chief who tried to unite the tribes east of the

a. Aaron Burr.
b. John Quincy Adams.
c. Oliver Hazard Perry.
d. Tecumseh.
e. John Marshall.
f. John Randolph of Roanoke.
g. William Henry Harrison.
h. Francis Scott Key.
i. Thomas Jefferson.
j. Andrew Jackson.

Mississippi in a
confederation.

5. ____ The governor of
Indiana Territory who
helped shatter the
Indian confederation.

6. ____ The naval officer who
helped the American
forces regain Lake Erie
during the War of
1812.

7. ____ The author of the
words to "The Star-
Spangled Banner."

8. ____ The American general
who defeated the
British at the Battle of
New Orleans.

9. ____ The secretary of state
who helped formulate
the Transcontinental
Treaty and the
Monroe Doctrine.

10. ____ The president who
sponsored the
Embargo Act to keep
the country out of war.

Multiple Choice

1. Aaron Burr was involved with each of these *except:*
   a. the "Northern Confederacy" in 1804.
   b. General James Wilkinson in the West.
   c. the Yazoo land frauds.
   d. a treason trial.

2. The order "No ship shall clear from the United States for any foreign port. No ship shall depart even for another American port without giving bond . . . that the goods will be relanded within the United States" is part of the:
   a. Berlin Decree.
   b. Embargo Act.
   c. Nonintervention Act.
   d. Macon's Bill No. 2.
3. Which of the following was a factor in the American decision to declare war on Great Britain in 1812?
   a. British Orders in Council.
   b. conflict between the British and Americans on the frontier.
   c. impressment.
   d. all of these.
4. The Hartford Convention was attended by:
   a. Federalists.
   b. Republicans.
   c. War Hawks.
   d. Jacksonians.
5. An Anglo-American rapprochement referred to:
   a. quasi-war between the countries.
   b. reestablishment of cordial relations.
   c. abrogation of previous treaties.
   d. détente.

ANSWERS
Matching: 1. f 2. a 3. e 4. d 5. g 6. c 7. h 8. j 9. b 10. i
Multiple Choice: c, b, d, a, b

8 / THE CORDS OF UNION

CHAPTER CHECKLIST

JAMES MONROE (1758–1831), 5th President

Born in Virginia and studied law with Thomas Jefferson.
United States senator from Virginia.
Minister to France.
Governor of Virginia.
Helped negotiate the Louisiana Purchase.
Secretary of state and then secretary of war under Madison.
President (1817–1825).
"Era of Good Feelings" was term used to describe his
   presidency.
Last of the "Virginia dynasty" presidents.

Sections of the Country

Northeast. The area north and east of Maryland was bound by a common concern with manufacturing.

South. There was a common bond of slavery and the agricultural staples, especially cotton.

West. The region between the Appalachian Mountains and the Mississippi River was a varied, changing zone which was not as cohesive politically as the other two sections.

Sectional Political Issues of the 1820s

Tariff. A tax on imports designed to protect domestic industries from foreign competition. The manufacturing North favored high protective tariffs, although New England shipping interests preferred free trade. Southerners rejected protection. It not only made their purchases higher at home, but they feared other countries would retaliate by placing tariffs on products such as cotton and tobacco which the South needed to sell to them.

National banking policy. The second Bank of the United States was authorized in 1816 with a 20-year charter. Sectional lines were not sharply drawn on this issue. More northern congressmen voted against the new Bank than for it; southern congressmen supported it, as did westerners, although the West opposed the Bank after the Panic of 1819.

Land policy. The West wanted public land to be sold cheaply. The North and South felt the government should get as much cash from it as possible. Northern manufacturers feared cheap western land would drain off surplus labor and force rates up. Southern planters were concerned about competition which would develop from cotton being grown in the Southwest.

Slavery. As the nation expanded, free and slave states were added in equal numbers. In 1819 there were 22 states, 11 free and 11 slave. In general, the North opposed slavery, the South favored the "peculiar institution." The West leaned toward the southern point of view.

Northern Leaders

Daniel Webster (1782–1852). Practiced law and entered politics both in his native New Hampshire and in Massachusetts. In Congress he was known as a great orator and as a representative of the business interests of New England. He was opposed to high tariffs, cheap land, federal construction of internal improvements, the establishment of the second Bank, and slavery. Basically he was a nationalist although he sometimes let the prejudices of New England obscure his feelings. See his picture on p. 233.

Martin Van Buren (1782–1862). A New York politician who never took a position if he could avoid doing so. Therefore, it is difficult to determine his views on the issues of the 1820s, except to say that he did not oppose internal improvements and that he did not conspicuously fight the rechartering of the Bank. Van Buren later became vice-president under Jackson and then president.

Southern Leaders

William H. Crawford (1772–1834). A Georgia conservative who served in the House, the Senate, as minister to France, and as secretary of the treasury under Monroe. He favored rechartering the Bank and supported a mildly protective tariff, although he was predisposed toward a states' rights position. His presidential ambitions were struck down in 1824 when he suffered a crippling stroke.

John C. Calhoun (1782–1850). A South Carolina politician who in the early 1820s was a true nationalist. He supported the national bank, a moderate tariff, and federal support of internal improvements. He served as congressman, as secretary of war under Monroe, and as vice-president under both Adams and Jackson. He was better known for his extreme states' rights position which he later proclaimed as senator from South Carolina. See his portrait on p. 235.

Western Leaders

Henry Clay (1777–1852). Practiced law in Kentucky and then became a congressman, serving as Speaker of the House from 1811 to 1820 and from 1823 to 1825. His nationalist view was bound up in a program he called the "American System." This plan called for a program of federal aid in the construction of roads and canals, a protective tariff, and a national bank. Note his portrait on p. 236.

Thomas Hart Benton (1782–1858). Senator for 30 years from Missouri, who favored free homesteads for pioneers and an extensive, federally sponsored internal improvements program. He opposed the Bank, and although personally opposed to the tariff, he voted for it to protect Missouri's lead and furs.

William Henry Harrison (1773–1841). A military man who served in the House and the Senate for Ohio. During the Panic of 1819 he took an anti-Bank and pro-high-tariff stand. He later became president, dying after one month in office.

Andrew Jackson (1767–1845). A politician and military hero from Tennessee who did not express his views on most issues. His forceful personality and military reputation were his chief assets.

Sectionalism and Politics

MISSOURI

1819, Missouri Enabling Act. Introduced in Congress to provide for the admission of Missouri as a state. It did not pass.

Tallmadge Amendment. Introduced by New York Congressman James Tallmadge as an amendment to the Missouri Enabling Act. Its purpose was to prohibit more slaves being brought into Missouri and to provide that all slaves born there after it became a state would be freed at the age of 25. The vote was along sectional lines, and the amendment passed the House but was rejected by the Senate.

1820, Missouri Compromise. Missouri was admitted to the Union as a slave state and Maine separated from Massachusetts and entered as a free state, thus preserving the balance of free and slave states. Congress also adopted the proposal of Senator Jesse B. Thomas of Illinois whereby slavery was prohibited in all other parts of the Louisiana Purchase north of 36° 30' north latitude, that is, north of Missouri's southern boundary. See the map on p. 238.

ELECTION OF 1824

This election was the second time a presidential election was thrown into the House of Representatives. There were four candidates, all members of the Democratic Republican party: Andrew Jackson, John Quincy Adams, William Crawford, and Henry Clay. Jackson got the largest number of votes in the electoral college, but not a majority;

JOHN QUINCY ADAMS (1767–1848), 6th President

Born in Massachusetts; graduated from Harvard; and practiced law.

Served as Minister to the Netherlands, Prussia, and Russia.

Federalist senator from Massachusetts, then switched his party affiliation to Democratic Republican.

Helped negotiate the Treaty of Ghent.

Secretary of state under Monroe where he negotiated the Transcontinental Treaty and helped write the Monroe Doctrine.

President (1825–1829).

Helped form a new party called the National Republican party.

Member of the House of Representatives (1831–1848).

so the top three, Jackson, Adams, and Crawford, were voted on in the House of Representatives, each state having one vote. Henry Clay asked those states which had supported him to vote for John Quincy Adams, and Adams won. Jackson felt that the election had been stolen from him and immediately began campaigning for the 1828 race.

"Corrupt bargain." President Adams appointed Henry Clay as secretary of state, the position which had traditionally been the "stepping-stone to the presidency." The defeated Jackson then cried that there had been a "corrupt bargain" made, whereby Clay used his influence to get Adams elected; in return, he got the Cabinet position plus possible support in the future for the presidency.

New Elements in the Economy

Factory system. Effectively introduced in the United States by Samuel Slater, who manufactured cotton thread.

Assembly line system of production. Made possible by Eli Whitney's precise methods of manufacturing parts for rifles which made the parts interchangeable.

Automation. Oliver Evans made effective use of machines in flour milling. One man poured grain down the chute, the other headed, that is, put the top on, the barrel of flour. All intervening steps of weighing, cleaning, grinding, and packing were performed by machines.

Regularly scheduled steamboats. John Fitch first operated steamboats on the Mississippi in 1790. They helped bring the west into the national economy.

Cotton gin. Invention by Eli Whitney designed to separate seeds from the fiber; made possible large-scale cotton cultivation in the south and caused a revival of slavery.

Bank of the United States. Existed from 1791 to 1811 and from 1816 to 1836, and was an important source of credit for business transactions.

Corporation. A company chartered by the states with certain rights and duties. At this time only companies with semipublic "products," such as roads, canals, insurance companies, and waterworks were incorporated.

The Factory

Samuel Slater (1768–1835). He is credited with the first effective introduction of the factory system into the United States. He set up machines to make cotton thread in Pawtucket, Rhode Island, in 1790. Slater was a textile mechanic in England, and the British, in order to protect their textile industry, barred both the export of textile machinery and the emigration of textile workers. Slater, however, memorized the plans for the machines and secretly emigrated to the United States, where the Quaker merchant Moses Brown financed his construction of a cotton spinning mill. See the picture of the mill on p. 242.

Francis Cabot Lowell (1775–1817). He designed an efficient power loom and set up the Boston Manufacturing Company in Waltham, Massachusetts. Lowell headed a group of merchants called the Boston Associates, who, between 1813 and 1850, built a number of large factories that revolutionized textile production. They concentrated upon the mass production of a standardized product—cheap, durable cloth.

"Lowell System." The efficient system used by Lowell and the Boston Associates in manufacturing cloth. It combined machine production, large-scale operation, professional management, and centralized marketing. Even though its efficiency was obvious, most manufacturing in the first half of the 1800s was still done by local craftsmen and traveling artisans.

Labor

Artisans. Individual craftsmen who produced goods ranging from barrels to cigars to clocks. In Monroe's time the household—handicraft—mill complex was still dominant, with no real factories, except in the manufacture of textiles.

Slaves. The importance of slavery was revived by the increased production of cotton made possible by the cotton gin. See the chart "Cotton Production and Slave Population, 1800–1860" on p. 246.

Increased need for slaves. While visiting a plantation near Savannah, Georgia, in 1793, Eli Whitney invented the cotton gin which revolutionized the cotton business. With a machine which could separate the seeds from the lint, it became profitable to grow greenseed, or upland, cotton, and thus more slaves were needed to work the expanding cotton fields. Note the chart "Prices for Cotton and for Slaves, 1802–1860" on p. 249.

Importation of slaves. The Constitution prohibited the importation of slaves from outside the United States after 1808.

Interstate traffic in slaves. The importation of slaves into a state in order to sell them was prohibited by some states in the late 18th century. These laws were increasingly evaded, and by 1820 some states were changing their laws to permit interstate slave trade.

Free blacks

American Colonization Society. Founded in 1817 by whites to send free blacks to Africa if they wished to go. The society purchased land in Africa and established the Republic of Liberia. Only about 12,000 blacks emigrated, and the society's efforts declined rapidly after 1830.

Blacks in northern states. Free blacks were generally denied civil rights such as voting or testifying in court. They could not get decent jobs or housing, and they faced discrimination in hospitals, churches, restaurants, and public transportation.

Transportation

Roads. A network of roads was needed for trade to move from the Mississippi Valley to the eastern seaboard. Building decent roads across the Appalachian Mountains was difficult. Steep grades had to be reduced; drainage ditches were essential; and a firm foundation of stones topped with gravel was necessary.

Turnpikes. Roads, built either by private companies or by states, which charged a fee or toll for using them.

Internal improvements. The general term used in the early 1800s to refer to the upgrading of transportation facilities, such as roads and canals. Some felt it was unconstitutional for the national government to become involved in these projects.

Water. The cheapest form of transportation.

Steamboat. In 1807 on the Hudson River, Robert Fulton launched the *Clermont,* the first successful commercial steamboat. He was financed by Robert Livingston, and for a while they held a monopoly on steamboat trade in New York waters and on the lower Mississippi River. The steamboat made freight charges decline sharply. In addition it was a comfortable way for passengers to travel.

Canal. This form of artificial waterway was expensive to build but provided a cheap form of transportation. Goods were placed on barges drawn by mules walking on towpaths along the banks of the canal. The *Erie Canal* was built in 1817–1825 to link the Hudson River with the Great Lakes, and indirectly New York City with the midwest. Its construction was encouraged by DeWitt Clinton, and it cost over $7 million. It opened up trade to the midwest, it cemented New York City's position as the nation's leading port, and the success of the Erie sparked a nationwide canal-building boom. Note the map "Canals and Roads, 1820–1850" on pp. 254, 255.

Government and Business

Incorporation laws. When a group of investors wanted to form a corporation, they had to ask the state legislature to pass a law specifically for their company. In 1811 New York passed the first general incorporation law, permitting blanket authorizations, but other states did not follow suit until 1837.

Tax benefits. Manufacturers in some states received tax breaks. For example, a New York law of 1817 exempted mills from taxation.

Patent Office. Created in 1790 to protect inventors. If a person tried to pirate a registered patent, he was subject to prosecution by the law.

Supreme Court Decisions

John Marshall. Chief justice from 1801 to 1835. His decisions reflected his belief in a strong central government and a national view of economic affairs. See Marshall's portrait on p. 258.

1819, *Sturges* v. *Crowninshield.* Upheld the importance of contracts. This decision declared a New York bankruptcy law unconstitutional because the state had applied the law to debts incurred before the law was passed. Debts were considered contracts.

1819, *Dartmouth College* v. *Woodward.* Stated that a charter granted by the state was a contract and could not be altered or canceled without the consent of both parties. The state of New Hampshire tried to change Dartmouth from a private to a public institution, but the Supreme Court said that it could not alter the charter granted to the college by the king in 1769.

1819, *McCulloch* v. *Maryland.* Asserted the supremacy of the federal government over the state governments. The state of Maryland had placed a tax on the bank notes of all banks not chartered by the state. This law was designed to tax the second Bank of the United States, which had a branch in Baltimore. In this decision, Chief Justice Marshall justified the constitutionality of the Bank and indicated that the state could not tax it.

1824, *Gibbons* v. *Ogden.* A decision which consolidated national power over commerce by regulating interstate trade. The decision destroyed the steamboat monopoly on the Hudson River held by Aaron Ogden of New York. It proclaimed that a state could regulate trade within its borders, but when part of the river's banks were shared with another state, in this case New Jersey, the national government or court had jurisdiction. The Supreme Court ruled against this monopoly.

1837, Charles River Bridge case. A decision of the Supreme Court under the new Chief Justice, Roger Taney, which, like Marshall's decisions, aided economic development. A free, state-owned bridge between Boston and Cambridge drew business from an older privately-owned toll bridge, and the private investors sued for damages. The Court ruled that the state had the right to place the "comfort and convenience" of the whole community over that of a particular company.

OTHER TERMS TO IDENTIFY

Era of Good Feelings. A phrase used to describe the period from 1817 to 1825 when James Monroe was president. There was only one political party at this time, the Democratic Republican, and Monroe tried to woo formerly Federalist New England by making a goodwill tour early in his administration. Monroe was greeted enthusiastically, and a Federalist newspaper, the *Columbian Centinel* in Boston, remarked on this new political unity by calling the times the "Era of Good Feelings." This phrase is not entirely accurate, however, for it was also a time of sectional and personal controversy.

William Jones. President of the second Bank of the United States from 1816 to 1819. Jones' easygoing management practices and the Bank's overextension of credit caused the institution trouble when the Panic of 1819 struck and Jones resigned.

Langdon Cheves. Second president of the second Bank of the United States. He was considered a conservative, and he cut back on credit extended at a time when, because of the panic, easy credit was needed. The Bank reached a low point in public favor.

Albany Regency. A term for the political machine in the state of New York which was controlled by Martin Van Buren.

Tapping Reeve's Law School. Founded in Litchfield, Connecticut, in 1784, its graduates included a number of men prominent in public affairs. John C. Calhoun was one.

Liberia. A country whose name means "place of freedom," founded on the west coast of Africa by the American Colonization Society. The purpose of the Society was to encourage slaveholders to free their slaves, and in 1820 it sent 88 blacks along with several white associates to this area in Africa which the members had purchased. In 1822 the settlers founded Monrovia, named after the United States president, which is today the capital of the country. In 1847 the colony broke its ties with the American Colonization Society and set up an independent republic with a government modeled on that of the United

States. Today in Liberia the ruling class is largely composed of the descendants of the freed slaves who colonized the area, while much of the population still follows its traditional tribal way of life.

Old National Road. Constructed by the national government from 1811 to 1818, it ran from Cumberland, Maryland, to Wheeling, in what is now West Virginia. It was gradually extended as far west as Vandalia, Illinois, by 1852. Note the map "Canals and Roads, 1820–1850" on pp. 254–255. Although some felt that even major interstate arteries should be financed by states and not by the federal government, this project continued and became the most important east-west land route between the Ohio Valley and the East.

Robert Fulton (1765–1815). Artist, engineer, inventor who spent 20 years in Europe, principally London and Paris, where he studied painting and invented a number of mechanical devices. His inventions included a power shovel for digging canals, a rope twister, designs for cast-iron bridges, a submarine, and a self-propelled submarine torpedo. His most famous design was the *Clermont,* the first successful commercial steamboat. See his portrait on p. 252.

DeWitt Clinton (1769–1828). A reform-minded politician who was mayor of New York City from 1803 to 1815 and governor of the state from 1817 to 1821 and from 1825 to 1828. He fought for free public education, education of women, and aid for minorities such as blacks and Indians. He is most famous for sponsoring the Erie Canal, which some of his opponents called "Clinton's Big Ditch."

GLOSSARY

bank notes.   A form of paper money, printed and issued by a specific bank. The bank promised to exchange the note for specie, that is, gold and silver, on demand. If a bank printed too many notes, and if a shaky economy caused too many depositors to convert them to hard money, then a bank might have to close its doors or temporarily suspend specie payments.

closed shop.   A business where employees are required to be union members before being hired. In general, judges at this time ruled against unions that tried to establish the closed shop.

delta.   The area near the mouth of a river where soil deposits are left by the wash of the river. It is usually triangular in shape and thus derives its name from delta, the fourth letter of the Greek alphabet, which is in the shape of a triangle. After the War of 1812, the delta region along the lower Mississippi River became important as a cotton raising area.

mulatto.   A person of mixed white and black ancestry.

prima facie.   A Latin phrase which literally means "on first appearance." It can also be interpreted as "at first sight" or "before closer inspection."

spinning jenny.   An early form of spinning machine on which a number of threads could be spun at once. It was invented about 1767 by James Hargreaves, an

English weaver, and consisted of a number of spindles turned by a common wheel worked by hand. A spindle is a rod which holds the spool of thread.

WORDS TO KNOW

Define the following, using the dictionary if necessary.

bard   manumission
chicanery   repine
inviolable   rhetorical
libertarian   towpath

SAMPLE QUESTIONS

Matching

1. _____ The phrase used by disgruntled Jacksonians after Adams appointed Clay as secretary of state.

2. _____ The term for a tax on imports.

3. _____ A period of time in which there was little strife between political parties.

4. _____ The term for a company which only hired workers who belonged to a labor union.

5. _____ A term referring to the construction of turnpikes and canals.

6. _____ A movement to send free blacks to Africa.

a. tariff.
b. Lowell System.
c. factory.
d. corporation.
e. closed shop.
f. colonization.
g. internal improvements.
h. Era of Good Feelings.
i. peculiar institution.
j. corrupt bargain.

7. _____ The machine
production of textiles
on a large scale with
centralized marketing
procedures.

8. _____ A company which
received a charter from
a state government.

9. _____ A building where
machines and laborers
came together under
one roof to make a
product.

10. _____ A term, often used by
southerners, to refer to
slavery.

Multiple Choice

1. The "Era of Good Feelings" witnessed the disappearance of which
   one of the following political parties?
   a. The Republican party.
   b. The Democratic Republican party.
   c. The Federalist party.
   d. The Whig party.
2. The status of slavery in the Louisiana Territory was affected by
   the:
   a. Missouri Compromise.
   b. Maine Compromise.
   c. American System.
   d. Jim Crow laws.
3. Which of the following pairs is incorrect?
   a. Eli Whitney: cotton gin.
   b. Samuel Slater: steamboat.
   c. Francis Cabot Lowell: power loom.
   d. Oliver Evans: flour-milling machine.
4. The purpose of the American Colonization Society was:
   a. to settle Americans west of the Appalachian Mountains.
   b. to bring over Irish to help build the Erie Canal.
   c. to send freed slaves to Africa.
   d. to remove Indians from Spanish Florida.

5. The principal trend in Supreme Court decisions while John Marshall was chief justice was:
   a. to weaken the position of the federal courts in the national government.
   b. to expand the powers of the national government.
   c. to strengthen the power of the states at the expense of the national government.
   d. to make the western states subordinate to those of the east.

9 / JACKSONIAN DEMOCRACY

CHRONOLOGY

1828	Tariff of Abominations
1828	*South Carolina Exposition and Protest*
1830	Webster-Hayne debate in Senate
1830	Maysville Road veto
1832	*Worcester* v. *Georgia*
1832	Veto of Bank rechartering.
1832–1833	South Carolina nullification controversy
1834	Whig Party established
1836	Specie Circular

CHAPTER CHECKLIST

TARIFF

1828, Tariff of Abominations. Northern and western agricultural interests were able to push through a bill placing high duties on raw wool, hemp, flax, fur, and liquor. The southerners unsuccessfully tried to block the bill and in their anger dubbed it the Tariff of Abominations.

1828, South Carolina Exposition and Protest. Written by John C. Calhoun to condemn the tariff and the economic ruin it could bring to the South. The essay is significant because in it Calhoun presented the idea that since the states had created the Union, they should have the final say as to the meaning of the Constitution. If a special state convention, representing the people, decided that an act of Congress violated the Constitution, that state could "nullify" the law within its boundaries. Four years later South Carolina tried to nullify the tariff.

> **ANDREW JACKSON (1767–1845), 7th President**
>
> Born in South Carolina and moved to Tennessee, where he
> practiced law.
> Nicknamed "Old Hickory," and his Tennessee plantation was
> called the Hermitage.
> Served as congressman and senator from Tennessee, and as a
> judge on the Tennessee Supreme Court.
> The hero of the Battle of New Orleans in the War of 1812.
> Invaded Florida during the Seminole War of 1818, and in 1821
> was appointed military governor of Florida.
> Won the popular vote in the presidential race of 1824, but lost
> the election in the House of Representatives.
> Formed a new political party, which he called the Democratic
> party.
> President (1829–1837).

The Jackson Era

Spoils system. Practice by which political party supporters were rewarded with government jobs. As William Marcy of New York proclaimed in 1831, "To the victors belong the spoils." Other presidents had appointed political friends to offices, but Jackson did so on a larger scale, replacing about 20 percent. He used a democratic justification for his actions—by "rotating" jobholders more citizens had an opportunity to participate in self-government. See the cartoon on p. 268.

Kitchen Cabinet. A group of unofficial advisers upon whom Jackson relied for advice, particularly between 1829 and 1831. The only member who was also part of the regular Cabinet was Martin Van Buren, who was secretary of state during Jackson's first term.

Webster-Hayne debate in the Senate

Senator Foot of Connecticut suggested the sale of public land should be sharply reduced.

Senator Benton of Missouri denounced this proposal as a plot by the eastern manufacturers to stop the westward migration of their workers.

Senator Hayne of South Carolina supported Benton and suggested that the West and the South work together to obtain cheap land and low tariffs.

Senator Webster of Massachusetts, who supported the northeastern manufacturers, spoke against Hayne's ideas.

1830, Webster-Hayne debate. Started as a discussion of federal land policies but ended as a debate of the states' rights versus the power of the national government. Hayne, voicing Vice-President Calhoun's views, spoke for states' rights while Webster, in a two-day oration, denounced nullification as close to treason. The ultimate effect prevented a West-South alliance. Note the picture on p. 270.

Indian problems. Jackson demonstrated a states' rights position by encouraging Georgia to ignore or "nullify" a Supreme Court decision concerning Indians.

Cherokee Nation. A tribe of Indians who tried to hold on to their land in Georgia by adopting white ways. They took up farming and cattle-raising, developed a written language, wrote a constitution, and set up a state within a state in Georgia.

1828. Georgia passed a law declaring all Cherokee laws void and the region part of Georgia.

1832, *Worcester* v. *Georgia.* A case involving missionaries, including Samuel Worcester, who had lived in the Cherokee territory without obtaining licenses required by the Georgia government. The Supreme Court ruled that the Cherokee tribe was a nation under the protection of the United States and therefore free from the jurisdiction of the state of Georgia. The president is responsible for enforcing Supreme Court decisions, but Jackson chose not to do so in this case.

In another case, a Cherokee named Corn Tassel was convicted in Georgia of a murder committed within the Cherokee territory. The Supreme Court ruled that he should not have been prosecuted in a Georgia court, but President Jackson refused to enforce the decision and Corn Tassel was hanged in Georgia.

1838–1839, Trail of Tears. A government order moved 15,000 Cherokees from Georgia to Oklahoma. About 4,000 died as a result of the forced emigration. See the map "Indian Removals" on p. 272.

Nullification crisis. Jackson took a nationalist rather than a states' rights position when South Carolina tried to nullify the tariff.

1828. The high Tariff of Abominations went into effect, and the South Carolina legislature passed eight resolutions denouncing it as unfair and unconstitutional.

1828. *South Carolina Exposition and Protest* was written by John C. Calhoun to oppose the tariff and to present an argument for a state's right to reject or "nullify" an act of Congress.

1832. Another tariff was passed which was also unsatisfactory to the South, particularly South Carolina.

November 1832. South Carolina elected a special convention which passed an Ordinance of Nullification, prohibiting the collection of tariff duties in the state after February 1, 1833. In January this deadline was postponed pending the outcome of the new tariff debate.

January 1833, Force Bill. Introduced to authorize President Jackson to call up troops if necessary to collect the tariff. The bill became law on March 1, but by then a compromise had been reached.

March 1833. A compromise tariff worked out by Henry Clay and John C. Calhoun passed Congress and provided for a gradual reduction over a 10-year period.

March 15, 1833. South Carolina convention reassembled and repealed the Nullification Ordinance, but, in order to save face, on the same day it adopted a new ordinance nullifying the Force Act.

Bank War

1816. Second Bank of the United States was chartered for a 20-year period.

1823. Nicholas Biddle, a wealthy Philadelphian, became president of the Bank. See his portrait on p. 276.

1832. Congress passed a bill to recharter the Bank, four years before its charter would have expired. This was a political move designed by the National Republicans to create an issue for the 1832 presidential campaign.

1832. Jackson vetoed the rechartering of the Bank. Although it continued in existence until 1836, Jackson won the "Bank war" by having federal income deposited in state banks, while he continued to draw money out of the national bank.

1836. Specie Circular provided that purchasers must pay for public land in gold or silver, rather than in bank notes. It was an effort by President Jackson to check inflation and land speculation. But it also set off a chain of events which led to the financial Panic of 1837. See the chart on p. 280.

Political Party Alignments

Democratic party. After the election of 1824, in which all candidates considered themselves Republicans (or Democratic Republicans as Jefferson had originally called the party), the followers of President Adams called themselves National Republicans. Jackson and his followers claimed to be the true political descendants of Jefferson, and they went back to the original name of the party, calling themselves Democrats. They shared some characteristics:

Personally loyal to Andrew Jackson.

Opposed the second Bank of the United States.

Supported states' rights, but also felt the union was supreme, as Jackson demonstrated in the nullification crisis.

Favored internal improvements, but felt they should be paid for by the state, as was evident in the Maysville Road veto.

Believed that the ordinary man was capable of performing the duties of most public offices. This view contributed to rotation in office, or the spoils system.

Championed a belief in the equality of all white men, which caused immigrants, Catholics, and other minority groups to join the party.

MAJOR POLITICAL PARTIES
AND APPROXIMATE DATES

------ Denotes a close relationship, but not direct evolution.
_____ Denotes direct evolution.

Whig party. Composed of the opponents of Andrew Jackson, whom they referred to as "King Andrew." They took their name from the Whig party in England, which traditionally supported a strong Parliament rather than a strong monarch. During the Revolution the Patriots had also called themselves Whigs, referring to their opposition to King George III.

Former Federalists and National Republicans began to call themselves Whigs in 1834.

Leaders included Henry Clay, Daniel Webster, and John C. Calhoun.

Favored the second Bank of the United States.

Wanted a national approach to economic problems, such as internal improvements.

Supported by the extreme states' rights followers of Calhoun.

Included people of education, culture, and social position.

Supported by voters predisposed to favor strong governments which would control the "excesses" of some individuals.

Had difficulty agreeing on anything other than opposition to Jackson.

MARTIN VAN BUREN (1782–1862), 8th President

Born in New York and studied law.

Called the "Red Fox" and the "Little Magician."

State senator and attorney general in New York.

Leader of the Albany Regency, the Democratic party machine of New York.

United States senator.

Won governorship of New York in 1828 and resigned to become Jackson's secretary of state.

Vice-president under Jackson (1833–1837).

President (1837–1841).

Van Buren's Policies

Fought the Bank of the United States as a monopoly, but also opposed irresponsible state banks.

Believed in public construction of internal improvements, but favored state rather than national programs.

Never committed himself on the tariff issue.

Generally followed states' rights rather than nationalist policies.

Took a hands-off approach to the depression which followed the Panic of 1837.

Supported the Independent Treasury Act which Congress passed in 1840. It called for the construction of government-owned vaults where all federal revenues could be stored until needed, rather than keeping them in state banks. To ensure absolute safety, all payments to the government were to be made in hard cash.

Election of 1840

Democrats nominated the incumbent, Martin Van Buren, but the years of depression and the stories told by his opponents led to his defeat. Van Buren was pictured by the Whigs as an extravagant man luxuriating in Washington, D.C., at the expense of the people.

Whigs nominated General William Henry Harrison, the well-educated son of a former governor of Virginia, and pictured him as a man of the people who lived in a log cabin and drank hard cider. They appealed to the western vote by recalling his Indian fighting days with the slogan "Tippecanoe and Tyler too." John Tyler of Virginia was the vice-presidential candidate.

General Harrison and the Whigs won the election by using the same appeal to the common man that the Democrats had used in electing Jackson. See the graph on p. 282.

WILLIAM HENRY HARRISON (1773–1841), 9th President

Born in Virginia, but moved West and became an Indian fighter.

Delegate to Congress from the Northwest Territory.

Governor of Indiana Territory from 1800 to 1813.

Led a force against an Indian encampment at Tippecanoe in 1811 and won the nickname "Old Tippecanoe."

Moved to Ohio and represented that state first in the House and then in the Senate.

President (1841).

Died from pneumonia on April 4, exactly one month after he had been inaugurated. He was the first president to die while in office.

OTHER TERMS TO IDENTIFY

Congressional caucus. The members of Congress met, by party, to select the presidential candidate for their party. This system came to an end before 1828. In that year Jackson and Adams were put forward by state legislatures. Soon the system of nomination by national party convention, such as we have today, was adopted.

Pocket veto. In order for a bill to become a law, the president must sign it within 10 days or it goes into effect even without his signature. He may also veto the bill and send it back to the house where it originated. Within the last 10 days of a congressional session, the president may simply "put the bill in his pocket," neither signing or vetoing it, and it has the same effect as a veto. Jackson not only used the veto more than all his predecessors combined but was also the first to use the pocket veto.

1828–1829, Eaton affair. Senator John Eaton of Tennessee, a bachelor, lived in a boardinghouse in Washington, D.C., and had an affair with the innkeeper's daughter, Peggy O'Neal Timberlake. Mrs. Timberlake was married to a Navy purser who was frequently away on sea duty. When her husband died in 1828, she married Eaton, then the newly appointed secretary of war. Other Cabinet wives refused to accept Mrs. Eaton socially; they were led in their snubbings by the vice-president's wife, Floride Calhoun. Martin Van Buren, a widower, was the only Cabinet member who paid his respects to the couple. President Jackson, remembering the social slights to his own wife, Rachel, was furious at the other Cabinet members. This fracas had political repercussions in that it marked the beginnings of John C. Calhoun's decline in favor and the ascendancy of Van Buren, who succeeded Calhoun as Jackson's vice-president. The affair also caused Jackson to turn more to his personal friends, that is, the Kitchen Cabinet, for advice.

1830, Maysville Road veto. Congress passed a bill to construct a turnpike from Maysville to Lexington, Kentucky. Jackson vetoed the bill, claiming that the road was intrastate rather than interstate and therefore the state should pay for it, not the federal government. This action illustrated a states' rights rather than a nationalist approach to internal improvements.

Pet banks. After Jackson vetoed the rechartering of the second Bank of the United States in 1832, he began to phase out the Bank by depositing new federal money in certain state banks. This procedure was handled by his newly appointed secretary of the treasury, Roger B. Taney, who deposited the money in state banks which were politically sympathetic to Jackson. These favored banks became known as "pet banks."

Locofoco. The name of the radical wing of Jackson's Democratic party which particularly championed the rights of the common man. A locofoco was a type of match, and the name was first used when a group of New York Jacksonians used these matches to light candles when a conservative faction had tried to break up their meeting by turning off the gaslights.

Washington *Globe.* The Washington newspaper which actively supported Jackson's policies. The paper's motto was "That government is best which governs least."

GLOSSARY

abomination. Something that elicits great dislike or loathing. Southerners called the high tariff of 1828 a Tariff of Abominations.

daguerreotype. An early type of photograph which became popular in the 1840s. It was produced on a silver plate or a copper plate covered with silver and developed by mercury vapor. Note the daguerreotype of Martin Van Buren on p. 283.

Haman. A favored minister in the court of Xerxes I, or Ahasuerus as he is called in the Bible, who was king of Persia in the 5th century B.C. Haman commanded that all Jews in the kingdom be put to death, but Queen Esther interceded for her people and Haman was hanged on the gallows which had been set up for Mordecai, a Jew whom Haman particularly hated. Jackson threatened Calhoun that if South Carolina attempted to nullify a law he would "hang him as high as Haman."

hard cider. Cider is made from the juice of apples. When it ferments, and thus has an alcoholic content, it is called hard cider.

latchstring. A cord or string on a latch, either hanging on the outside of the door so that the latch can be raised from the outside, or drawn inside to prevent people from entering unless the door is opened from the inside. In the 1840 election, the Whigs stated that their candidate lived in a log cabin where the latchstring was always out, that is, welcoming everyone.

lithograph. A print made by the process of lithography. Lithography is a printing process in which the image to be printed is drawn on a flat surface, such as stone, or more recently on zinc or aluminum. The surface is treated so that the drawing will retain ink and the negative area is treated to repel ink. Note the lithograph on p. 273.

logrolling. Trading votes among legislators to achieve passage of laws of interest to one another. A good deal of logrolling occurred in Congress every time a new tariff bill came up, because legislators wanted the highest possible duties to protect industries in their own districts.

South Sea Bubble. The popular name in England for the financial speculation in the South Sea Company, which was formed in 1711 and failed disastrously in 1720. Needing money to finance the War of Spanish Succession, the British government allowed the company to assume the national debt in exchange for an annual interest payment from the government plus a monopoly of British trade with the islands of the South Seas and South America. The price of the stock rose out of all proportion to its earnings in trade, and eventually the stock collapsed and the bubble burst.

WORDS TO KNOW

Define the following, using the dictionary if necessary.

cordon	masthead (newspaper)
equivocate	munificent
hydra	specious
inexorable	tidewater

SAMPLE QUESTIONS

Matching

1. _____ The doctrine that a state government could declare an act of Congress unconstitutional.

2. _____ The first Whig to be elected as president.

3. _____ The first vice-president to become president because of the death of the incumbent president.

4. _____ President of the Second Bank of the United States in Philadelphia.

5. _____ Provided for the construction of government-owned vaults where federal revenues could be stored until needed.

6. _____ Secretary of the treasury who removed deposits from the national bank and placed them in "pet banks."

7. _____ Provided that purchasers must pay for public land in gold or silver.

a. John Tyler.
b. Specie Circular.
c. Nicholas Biddle.
d. William Henry Harrison.
e. nullification.
f. South Carolina.
g. Independent Treasury Act.
h. Georgia.
i. Roger Taney.
j. veto.

8. _____ This state would not recognize the Cherokee Indians' attempt to establish a sovereign nation within its boundaries.

9. _____ This state declared that it would not enforce the tariff act passed by Congress in 1832.

10. _____ The refusal of a president to sign a bill into law.

Multiple Choice

1. What was Andrew Jackson's attitude toward the spoils system?
   a. that civil service laws should be strengthened.
   b. that the spoils system was bad, but he could not do anything about it.
   c. that rotation in office was a good thing.
   d. that only highly educated persons should hold jobs in the government.
2. The South Carolina Ordinance of Nullification of 1832 expressed the ideas of:
   a. Daniel Webster
   b. Andrew Jackson
   c. John Adams
   d. John C. Calhoun
3. One result of the Peggy Eaton affair was:
   a. a victory for the Calhoun faction.
   b. a serious breach between Jackson and Calhoun.
   c. the resignation of the Kitchen Cabinet.
   d. Van Buren's fall from power.
4. Jackson's chief weapon in the "Bank War" was:
   a. removing Biddle from office.
   b. depositing government money in state banks.
   c. printing more money.
   d. issuing the Specie Circular.

5. Which of the following defended the view that the Union was formed by the whole people of the United States and not by the states?

   a. John C. Calhoun.
   b. Thomas Jefferson.
   c. Robert Hayne.
   d. Daniel Webster.

10 / THE MAKING OF MIDDLE-CLASS AMERICA

CHAPTER CHECKLIST

Alexis de Tocqueville (1805–1859). A French politician and writer who came to the United States in 1831 with a companion, Gustave de Beaumont, to study the prison system. However, their nine months of travel, commissioned by the French government but paid for by their families, gave them a broader view. Tocqueville wrote about his experiences in *Democracy in America,* a translation of the French version which had been published in 1834. See his portrait on p. 292.

Tocqueville's impressions:

- *"The whole society seems to have turned into one middle class."*
  Compared with Europe he saw fewer distinctions between the rich and the poor.
- *"A man builds his house . . . and sells it before the roof is on."*
  Americans were restless, and in particular, were moving westward.
- *"The whole society is a factory."*
  Almost all Americans worked for a living, and by the 1830s, many jobs were outside the home.

- *"A sort of equality reigns around the domestic hearth."*
  Since more men were working outside the home, women assumed more authority as they exercised day-to-day control over household affairs.
- *"The most religious country in the world."*
  Tocqueville witnessed the success of the evangelists of the Second Great Awakening.
- *"Americans of all ages . . . are forever forming associations."*
  Americans were "joiners" of groups which supported charities, reforms, and self-improvement.

Labor

Craftsman. His importance in the economy declined as a cheap, efficient product became more sought after than a finely finished one.
  Apprentice. An employee in training under a master craftsman from a period of five to seven years. Typically he slept in the shop, was often treated as a member of the family, and, if lucky, married the master's daughter and joined the business.
  Journeyman. In this intermediate status, the trained laborer worked for wages by the day. "Journeyman" is derived from the French *journée,* which means "day."
  Master. After demonstrating his ability by exam or by creating a "masterpiece," the laborer was considered a master craftsman and renewed the cycle by hiring his own apprentices.

Factory worker. Women and children took many of the factory positions because machines lessened the need for both strength and skill. By the early 1820s about half of the cotton textile workers were under age 16. In the 1830s, 85 percent of the textile mill work force were women. Note the picture on p. 297.
  "Waltham System." A system developed by the Boston Associates of employing unmarried girls and housing them in company dormitories. It was named after their Waltham, Massachusetts, textile mill.
  Immigrants. By the 1840s mill owners increasingly turned to Irish immigrants to tend their machines, and women found positions instead as school teachers or clerks. See the chart "Immigration, 1820–1860" on p. 295.

Religion

Second Great Awakening. A religious revival movement which reached its crest in the early 1830s. It was similar in its emotional approach to the original Great Awakening of the 1740s.

Charles Grandison Finney (1792–1875). A lawyer turned preacher whose most successful religious revivals were along the Erie Canal between 1826 and 1831. Finney consciously "worked up" the crowds by soliciting personal testimonies and providing "anxious benches" where individuals waited to hear God's call from within before coming forward to declare themselves saved. First a Presbyterian, then a Congregationalist, Finney later taught at Oberlin College in Ohio and was its president from 1851 to 1865. See his picture on p. 303.

Rappites. Followers of the religious leader George Rapp (1757–1847), who left Germany with 600 people and founded a religious community in 1804 near Pittsburgh. The Rappites believed that the millennium, or the second coming of Jesus followed by the end of the world, was about to happen. Therefore, everyone should be prepared. The group worked their land communally, shared the produce, and practiced celibacy.

Shakers. Members of a religious movement founded by Ann Lee (1736–1784), who by the 1830s had established about 20 communities where they could practice their beliefs. Like the Rappites, the Shakers held property in common, practiced celibacy, and believed the millennium was imminent. Officially named the United Society of Believers in Christ's Second Coming, they got the name Shaker from their early custom of dancing with shaking movements during ceremonies.

Mormons. Members of a new religion founded by Joseph Smith in the 1820s, officially named the Church of Jesus Christ of Latter Day Saints. The Mormons had a flourishing settlement in Nauvoo, Illinois, from 1839, (see picture on p. 306) but then in 1847, because of the resentment of their non-Mormon neighbors, they moved further west to Utah under the leadership of Brigham Young. Characteristics of the early church were a strong sense of community cooperation and the practice of polygamy; that is, a man could have more than one wife.

Reform Movements

PRISON

Philadelphia System. A prison system based on strict solitary confinement so that prisoners could reflect on their wrongdoings and, it was hoped, reform their ways.

Auburn System. A prison system developed in New York State which allowed some social contact and work in shops and stone quarries. Absolute silence was required, and whippings were administered for the slightest breaking of the rules.

MENTAL HOSPITALS

Dorothea Dix (1802–1887). A reformer who persuaded the Massachusetts legislature and then other states to improve the care of the mentally ill. In her surveys she found that people with mental problems were often held in prisons and jails, and her efforts were instrumental in the establishment of 32 state mental hospitals. See her picture on p. 307.

TEMPERANCE

American Temperance Union. Founded in 1826, the Union started a crusade to get people to "sign the pledge" not to drink alcoholic beverages. The word *temperance* usually means "moderation," but the primary goal of the Temperance Union was to persuade people to abstain completely from drinking liquor. Another goal was to prohibit by law the sale of alcoholic beverages, and in 1846 Maine became the first state to pass such legislation. The prohibition movement culminated in 1919 with the passage of the Eighteenth Amendment to the Constitution prohibiting the sale of liquor. This amendment was reversed in 1933 with the Twenty-first Amendment.

ABOLITION

Benjamin Lundy (1789–1839). A Quaker and editor of the Baltimore-based newspaper, *The Genius of Universal Emancipation.* He urged the use of persuasion in the South rather than interference by the federal government, and he promoted colonization of free blacks in Africa.

William Lloyd Garrison (1805–1879). An extremist leader of the abolition movement who called for an immediate, rather than a gradual, end to slavery. Garrison established a newspaper, *The Liberator* (1831–1865), to spread his message; he also founded several antislavery societies. He was considered one of the most radical and uncompromising of the abolitionists. See his picture on p. 310.

Theodore Dwight Weld (1803–1895). A minister dedicated to the emancipation, or freeing, of slaves. He was willing to accept a more gradual approach than was Garrison. Weld used an emotional appeal and was active in the abolitionist movement in the 1830s.

Arthur and Lewis Tappan. New York businessmen who subsidized Garrison's *The Liberator* and then turned their support to the evangelist Weld and to the organization of the Liberty party.

James G. Birney (1792–1857). Originally a Kentucky slaveholder, he later became executive secretary of the American Anti-Slavery Society and was the presidential candidate of the Liberty party in 1840 and 1844.

Frederick Douglass (1817–1895). A slave who escaped to the North and became an abolitionist leader. He gave antislavery lectures in the

United States and Great Britain, wrote a moving autobiography, *Narrative of the Life of Frederick Douglass* (1845), and in 1847 founded *The North Star,* an abolitionist newspaper. Douglass and Weld were willing to work within the governmental structure to obtain change, whereas Garrison once burned a copy of the Constitution to show his disdain for a system which allowed slavery. See the picture of Douglass on p. 311.

WOMEN'S RIGHTS

Elizabeth Cady Stanton (1815–1892). An abolitionist who turned to women's rights when she attended the World Antislavery Convention in London in 1840 and found that women were not allowed to participate in the debates. She helped organize the Seneca Falls Convention in 1848, and in 1869 the National Woman Suffrage Association elected her president, an office she held for 21 years. The suffrage movement campaigned for women's right to vote, and it was eventually successful at the national level in 1920 with the passage of the Nineteenth Amendment. See Stanton's picture on p. 313.

1848, Seneca Falls Convention. A meeting in Seneca Falls, New York, which began the women's rights movement in the United States. It was organized by Elizabeth Cady Stanton and Lucretia Mott, and about 300 people, including 40 men, gathered to hear a Declaration of Principles based on the Declaration of Independence.

Susan B. Anthony (1820–1906). A reformer who was primarily known as a campaigner for women's rights, although she was also active in abolitionist and temperance societies. She was a close associate of Elizabeth Cady Stanton in the suffrage movement.

OTHER TERMS TO IDENTIFY

Frances Trollope (1780–1863). An English woman who lived in Cincinnati, Ohio, from 1829 to 1832 and wrote an unflattering view in *Domestic Manners of Americans* (1832). She told her English readers that Americans were just as uncouth as they had imagined.

Horace Greeley (1811–1872). The editor of the New York *Tribune* who wrote "Go West, young man, and grow up with the country." The quotation appeared in *Hints Toward Reforms* (1850), a collection of Greeley's lectures.

Calvinism. Refers to the teachings of John Calvin (1509–1564), a French Protestant theologian of the Reformation whose views were reflected, especially in the Congregational (Puritan) and the Presbyterian churches. Some of his doctrines included predestination and infant damnation, which stated that only those who had been preordained, or "elected," by God to be saved would go to heaven. One's desire to convert or a baby's lack of opportunity to sin personally were not factors in salvation. These strict doctrines were set aside in the United States during the Second Great Awakening.

Brook Farm. A utopian community which existed from 1841 to 1847 in Massachusetts. Founded by George Ripley, the settlement became a retreat for transcendentalists. The farm was a communal society in which labor was shared.

Charles Fourier (1772–1837). A French utopian socialist who believed that the natural inclinations of man, if properly channeled, would result in social harmony. Society should be organized into phalanxes, or economic units composed of 1,620 people in each. People would live in a community building and divide the work among them. In the 1840s several dozen Fourierist colonies were established in the United States; none lasted very long.

Thomas Hopkins Gallaudet (1787–1851). Founder of the first free school for the deaf in 1817 in Hartford, Connecticut. His youngest son started the school which became Gallaudet College for the Deaf in Washington, D.C.

Sarah (1792–1873) and Angelina Grimké (1805–1879). Members of a slaveholding South Carolina family, these two sisters moved north, joined the Quakers, and became active in the abolitionist and women's rights movements.

GLOSSARY

atheism.   Disbelief or denial of the existence of God. Robert Owen, the British utopian socialist who bought the Rappite settlement at New Harmony, Indiana, advocated "enlightened atheism," a stand which made him unpopular with the religious majority in nearby communities.

brogan.   A heavy, ankle-high work shoe. The growing shoe industry in the early 1800s concentrated on producing rough brogans for slaves and western farmers, rather than on making finely crafted shoes which required more skill.

chauvinist.   One who is militant or boastful concerning a particular cause. The term was named after Nicholas Chauvin, a French soldier who was extremely devoted to Napoleon.

communitarian.   A member or supporter of a community in which there are no social classes and in which there is common ownership of the means of production. The Rappites and the Shakers were communitarians.

gentile.   One who is not of the Jewish faith, particularly a Christian as distinguished from a Jew. Among Mormons, however, a gentile is any person who is not a Mormon.

Industrial Revolution.   A term referring to the transformation of a society from basically agricultural and commercial to one in which factories and complex machines are vital. Industrialization began in Great Britain in the 1700s but did not fully take place in the United States until after the Civil War.

millennium.   In Christian tradition, the millennium is a 1,000-year period of holiness in which Christ is to rule on earth. Both the Rappites and the Shakers believed that the millennium was imminent.

proletariat.   Laborers who work for a wage, not having enough capital, or money, to go into business for themselves or to invest in someone else's business. Karl Marx (1818–1883), the German philosopher who is considered the founder of modern communism, referred to the working class as the proletariat.

Zion.   A place or community regarded as being especially devoted to God. The Mormons established their Zion on the shores of the Great Salt Lake in Utah.

WORDS TO KNOW

Define the following, using the dictionary if necessary.

adamant	grog
amalgamation	itinerant
braggadocio	manacled
cloying	prodigious

SAMPLE QUESTIONS

Matching

1. ____ Leader of the Mormons when they moved to Utah.

2. ____ A slave who became an abolitionist leader.

3. ____ A reformer who improved conditions for the mentally ill.

4. ____ Editor of *The Liberator.*

5. ____ Organizer of the Seneca Falls Convention in 1848.

6. ____ Founder of the Mormon Church.

7. ____ Founder of the Shakers.

a. Alexis de Tocqueville.
b. Charles Grandison Finney.
c. Ann Lee.
d. Joseph Smith.
e. Dorothea Dix.
f. Brigham Young.
g. James Birney.
h. William Lloyd Garrison.
i. Frederick Douglass.
j. Elizabeth Cady Stanton.

8. _____ Evangelist of the
Second Great
Awakening.

9. _____ Author of *Democracy
in America.*

10. _____ Presidential candidate
of the Liberty party.

Multiple Choice

1. In the 1830s a majority of the textile mill workers were:
   a. women.
   b. children.
   c. labor union members.
   d. immigrants.
2. Which one of the following pairs has the least in common?
   a. Ann Lee and Joseph Smith.
   b. Elizabeth Cady Stanton and Susan Anthony.
   c. Benjamin Lundy and Arthur Tappan.
   d. Sarah Grimké and Frances Trollope.
3. The Auburn System was an experiment in:
   a. insane asylums.
   b. penitentiary reform.
   c. labor unions for women textile workers.
   d. education for the blind.
4. The American Temperance Union was organized to:
   a. end child abuse.
   b. fund insane asylums.
   c. foster mercy to prison inmates.
   d. stop the consumption of alcoholic beverages.
5. The most influential black abolitionist was:
   a. Frederick Douglass.
   b. Theodore Weld.
   c. James Birney.
   d. William Lloyd Garrison.

ANSWERS
Matching: 1. f 2. i 3. e 4. h 5. j 6. d 7. c 8. b 9. a 10. g
Multiple Choice: a, d, b, d, a

11 / A DEMOCRATIC CULTURE

CHAPTER CHECKLIST

Romanticism. A 19th-century climate of opinion which emphasized feeling and intuition rather than thought and intellect. The importance of the individual and of nature was also stressed.

Literature

James Fenimore Cooper (1789–1851). A novelist who wrote a series of stories about Indians and settlers on the frontier, such as *The Spy* and *The Last of the Mohicans.* His stories reflected early 19th-century romanticism in which civilization was portrayed as corrupt and the Indian and his wilderness as noble and natural.

Washington Irving (1783–1859). An author who won acclaim in New York by writing the comical Diedrich Knickerbocker's *History of New York.* He then moved to Europe (1815–1832) where he wrote his most important book, The *Sketch Book of Geoffrey Crayon, Gent,* which included "Rip Van Winkle" and "The Legend of Sleepy Hollow."

Transcendentalism. A way of looking at life in which feelings were more important than facts and the individual was glorified. The literal meaning of the word is "to go beyond the world of the senses."

Ralph Waldo Emerson (1803–1882). A transcendentalist writer who gave up his pulpit as a Unitarian minister to become an essayist and lecturer. He encouraged other writers to seek inspiration in their own surroundings rather than in European models and thus to develop a national American literature. See his picture on p. 328.

Henry David Thoreau (1817–1862). A transcendentalist writer who from 1845 to 1847 lived at Walden Pond on Ralph Waldo Emerson's land and used it as a retreat from civilization. In 1854 he published *Walden,* which summarized his individualistic philosophy and his love of nature. Later he became involved in the antislavery movement. Note the photo of the pond on p. 329.

Edgar Allan Poe (1809–1849). A poet, critic, and short story writer who perfected the detective story, as in "The Murders in the Rue Morgue," and was a master of the horror tale, such as "The Pit and the Pendulum." His most famous poem, "The Raven," was published in 1845. Poe's personal life was chaotic. In 1849 he was found semiconscious in a Baltimore saloon and died four days later. See his portrait on p. 330.

Nathaniel Hawthorne (1804–1864). A Massachusetts writer who drew heavily on the Puritan heritage of New England in his works. His novels dealt with the individual's struggle with sin and guilt. This theme is evident in his most famous novels *The Scarlet Letter* (1850) and *House of the Seven Gables* (1851).

Herman Melville (1819–1892). A novelist who spent his early life at sea and his later life writing fictionalized accounts of his travels. His most famous novel was *Moby Dick,* published in 1851. Melville, like Hawthorne, had a dark view of human nature, unlike the idealism of the transcendentalists. In common with other romantic writers, however, both Melville and Hawthorne heeded Emerson's advice and pursued non-European themes.

Walt Whitman (1819–1892). A poet whose most famous work was a collection of poems entitled *Leaves of Grass.* The first edition appeared in 1848 and contained 12 poems. Whitman continued to add to the volume, and in 1860 *Leaves of Grass* had grown to 122 poems. The ninth and final edition appeared in 1892, the year of Whitman's death. See the daguerreotype of Whitman on p. 332.

POPULAR READING

Penny newspapers. Cheap news sheets which depended on sensation, crime stories, and society gossip to appeal to the masses. The first was the New York *Sun,* which was begun in 1833.

"Domestic" novels. Moralistic, sentimental stories whose themes were similar to those of today's soap operas.

Religious books. The American Tract Society was a group which published and distributed religious tracts. A tract is a pamphlet or booklet which makes a declaration or appeal, usually a religious or political one. The society did not promote the doctrines of any particular Christian denomination but sent out missionary-salesmen to preach the gospel and sell or give away religious books. The American Bible Society had similar goals and issued hundreds of thousands of copies of the Old and New Testaments of the Bible each year.

Architecture

Charles Bulfinch (1763–1844). An architect who studied in England and then developed his own "Federal" style, which was used most extensively in Boston. Note an example pictured on p. 334.

American Gothic. A style of architecture popular in the 19th century which often included towers, steeples, arches, and elaborate wood trim. The Smithsonian Institution in Washington, D.C., designed in 1846 by James Renwick, is a good example. The original Gothic architecture was used in western Europe from the 12th through the 15th centuries.

Art

TURN OF THE CENTURY

John Singleton Copley (1738–1815). An artist who developed a successful career in Boston as a portrait painter of wealthy New Englanders. His technique was sometimes criticized, however, so in 1774 he moved to London and continued his painting there. Note the portrait of Sam Adams by Copley on p. 110.

Charles Willson Peale (1741–1827). An artist who helped found the Pennsylvania Academy of Fine Arts and did much to encourage American painting. He also established in Philadelphia a museum of natural history, which contained fossils and stuffed animals. Note his portrait of his family on p. 326, or the painting of George Washington on p. 143.

Gilbert Stuart (1755–1828). An American artist best known for his portraits of George Washington. See his portrait of John Randolph of Roanoke on p. 204.

TOWARD THE MID-1800S

George Catlin (1796–1872). A painter and writer who specialized in the study of Indians and tribal life. He published his engravings in a number of books, including *Manners, Customs, and Condition of the North American Indians* (1841).

Genre painters. Artists whose paintings depicted scenes and subjects of everyday life. Their work was designed to appeal to the general public. See the picture by William Sidney Mount on p. 336.

Hudson River school. A group of artists who created large landscape paintings of America's countryside, particularly of the Hudson River valley in New York. About a dozen painters made up the group, and their canvases reflected the same concern with nature that the transcendentalists expressed in literature.

Currier and Ives. Printmakers who specialized in lithographs depicting American life, manners, and history. The firm operated by Nathaniel Currier (1813–1888) and James Merritt Ives (1824–1895) sold cheap prints in quantity, and from the 1850s brought this form of art into many American homes. See their print of a Mexican War battle on p. 357.

American Art-Union. A group in New York (1839–1851) formed to encourage native art. They sold what were in effect lottery tickets in order to purchase paintings, which became the prizes in the lottery. By 1849, nearly 19,000 subscribed to "memberships." By giving away thousands of engravings of its prize-winning paintings, the Art-Union brought competent American works of art into middle-class homes.

Education

Horace Mann (1796–1859). A pioneer in the reform of public education. He was the first secretary of the Massachusetts Board of Education (1837–1848) and urged such reforms as a minimum school year of six months and professional teacher training.

Henry Barnard (1811–1900). Promoted the common-school movement in Connecticut and Rhode Island and served as chancellor of the University of Wisconsin and as president of St. John's College in Annapolis. He became the first United States commissioner of education, and he edited the *American Journal of Education* from 1855 until 1882.

Common-school movement. A push for tax-supported, state-supervised public schools with well-trained teachers. Its premise was the belief that a government based on democratic rule required an educated public. By the 1850s every state outside the South provided free elementary schools, and a few states financed high schools and even colleges.

Francis Wayland (1769–1865). President of Brown University in Rhode Island from 1827 until 1855. His 1842 address, "On the Present Collegiate System," called for a change in the typical college curriculum from an emphasis on Latin, Greek, and Biblical studies to courses in science, economics, modern history, and applied mathematics.

Lyceums. Mutual improvement societies which might be compared to today's adult continuing education programs. The first lyceum was started in Massachusetts in 1826 by Josiah Holbrook. Soon there were thousands of these lecture and discussion clubs coordinated by the National American Lyceum, all over the United States.

Science

William Beaumont (1785–1853). A physician who, while serving as army post surgeon at Mackinac Island, was called upon in 1822 to treat 19-year-old Alexis St. Martin, whose abdomen had been torn open by an accidental gunshot wound. Although St. Martin recovered, the wound never completely closed, and Beaumont took advantage of the unusual situation to conduct over 200 experiments on the digestive process.

OTHER TERMS TO IDENTIFY

Benjamin West (1738–1820). An American-born artist who moved to Europe in 1760 and spent most of his life painting and teaching in England. He was influential in American painting of the period because a number of young artists from the United States studied under him, including John Singleton Copley, Charles Willson Peale, and Gilbert Stuart.

Henry Wadsworth Longfellow (1807–1882). A poet and professor of modern languages at Harvard who was famous for such poems as "The Village Blacksmith," "Paul Revere's Ride," and *The Song of Hiawatha.*

James Russell Lowell (1819–1891). A poet and literary critic who succeeded Longfellow as professor of modern languages at Harvard. His humorous satire can be seen in the *Biglow Papers*. Lowell became the first editor of the *Atlantic Monthly,* founded in Boston in 1857.

George Bancroft (1800–1891). An historian who is sometimes called the "father of American history" because of his 10-volume *History of the United States,* which was published between 1834 and 1874. Bancroft was also secretary of the navy, acting secretary of the army, and ambassador to Great Britain and Germany.

William Hickling Prescott (1792–1859). An historian who wrote extensively on Spain and her empire in America. His most famous works were *Conquest of Mexico* (1843) and *Conquest of Peru* (1847).

Francis Parkman (1823–1893). An historian who wrote about the struggle between France and Great Britain for the control of North America.

William Gilmore Simms (1806–1870). A southern writer of the romantic era whose favorite theme was the South Carolina frontier. Simms' works, along with those of John Pendleton Kennedy, another southern writer, contributed much to the glamorous legend of the Old South.

Maria Mitchell (1818–1889). American astronomer who was a school teacher and librarian in Nantucket, Massachusetts. She made a special study of sunspots and calculated the position of a comet in 1847. After 1865 she was a professor of astronomy at Vassar College. See her photo on p. 343.

GLOSSARY

backwater. A place regarded as backward or stagnant. Washington, D.C., was considered a cultural backwater. The original meaning referred to a body of still water held back by a dam or current.

bar. The railing in a courtroom enclosing the part of the room where the judges and lawyers sit, witnesses are heard, and prisoners are tried. Tocqueville reported, "At the bar or the bench the American aristocracy is found," referring to lawyers and judges.

colporteur. A person who sells or gives away religious literature. The term is derived from an Old French word *comporteur,* which means to peddle. The American Tract Society had hundreds of these missionary–salesmen.

coup. A brilliantly executed plan. The first Beethoven symphony ever heard in America was performed in Cincinnati, and as a result of such coups, the "Queen City" replaced Lexington, Kentucky, as the center of trans-Allegheny culture.

phrenology. The practice of studying a person's character and mental capabilities from the contours of the head. Different segments of the head supposedly control such characteristics as self-esteem, friendship, and hope.

physiologist. A scientist who studies the essential life processes and functions. Dr. William Beaumont's experiments won him a reputation among European physiologists as the world's leading expert on the human gastric system.

pirate. To reproduce the literary works of an author without permission. The works of English novelists were frequently pirated by American publishers.

printer's devil. An apprentice in a printing establishment. At age 13 Walt Whitman left school and became a printer's devil.

Smithsonian Institute. The national museum in Washington, D.C., founded in 1846. It was named after James Smithson (1765–1829), a British chemist and mineralogist who left a bequest to found such an institution. The original museum is in the American Gothic style, but the new addition completed in the 1960s is more modern. The Smithsonian is often referred to as "the nation's attic."

WORDS TO KNOW

Define the following, using the dictionary if necessary.

actuary	lugubrious
arbiters	omnivorously
charlatan	prodigality
juxtapose	vermilion

SAMPLE QUESTIONS

Matching

1. _____ Painter of Indians and of tribal life

2. _____ Architect who designed buildings in the Federal style

3. _____ Author of *Walden*

4. _____ Physician who researched the digestive system

5. _____ Writer who perfected the detective story

6. _____ First secretary of the Massachusetts school board

a. Josiah Holbrook.
b. Henry David Thoreau.
c. William Beaumont.
d. James Fenimore Cooper.
e. Walt Whitman.
f. Charles Willson Peale.
g. Charles Bulfinch.
h. George Catlin.
i. Edgar Allen Poe.
j. Horace Mann.

7. _____ Poet who wrote *Leaves of Grass*

8. _____ Novelist who wrote about Indians and frontier settlers

9. _____ Founder of the lyceum movement

10. _____ Artist who also opened a museum of natural history

Multiple Choice

1. An emphasis on emotion and feeling, optimism, and individualism were characteristics which best describe:
   a. phrenology.
   b. romanticism.
   c. physiology.
   d. the Hudson River school.

2. "That government is best which governs not at all," was a statement made by the individualist:
   a. Susan Warner.
   b. Henry Barnard.
   c. Josiah Holbrook.
   d. Henry David Thoreau.

3. Which one of the following was least significant in promoting American contributions to painting?
   a. American Art-Union.
   b. John Singleton Copley.
   c. Benjamin West.
   d. George Catlin.

4. The educator Horace Mann was most interested in the:
   a. common-school movement.
   b. Hudson River school.
   c. Smithsonian Institution.
   d. lyceum movement.

5. Which one of the following statements about higher education in Jacksonian America is incorrect?

a. the curriculum had almost no practical relevance except for future clergymen.

b. there were too many students and too few colleges.

c. college was beyond the economic means of the average family.

d. classwork standards were low.

ANSWERS
Matching: 1. h 2. g 3. b 4. c 5. i 6. j 7. e 8. d 9. a 10. f
Multiple Choice: b, d, c, a, b

12 / EXPANSION AND SLAVERY

CHAPTER CHECKLIST

JOHN TYLER (1790–1862), 10th President

Born in Virginia and educated at William and Mary.
Member of the House of Representatives (1817–1821).
Governor of Virginia (1825–1827).
United States senator (1827–1836).
Member of the Jeffersonian Republican party, then the Jacksonian Democratic party, then the Whig party.
Vice-president under William Henry Harrison during his one month in office.
President (1841–1845).

Tyler as President

States' rights view of the Constitution.
Opposed the Bank, a high tariff, and federal internal improvements,

all of which were supported by Henry Clay and the northern Whigs.

Cast out by party, he unsuccessfully tried to build a party of his own. See the picture of Tyler on p. 348.

1841, Distribution Act. A measure supported by Henry Clay, whereby the proceeds from the sale of public land went to the states. This act was designed to improve the financial situation of the states, but Clay also wanted to lower the amount in the national treasury so as to justify raising the tariff. The Distribution Act was repealed the next year.

1841, Preemption Act. Legalized the right of squatters to occupy unsurveyed public land and to buy it later at $1.25 an acre without bidding for it at auction.

Problems with England

Maine-New Brunswick boundary dispute. Became critical in 1838–1839 when Canadians began cutting timber in the Aroostook Valley, which was claimed by the United States. This action led to the Aroostook "war," a bloodless, undeclared war that threatened Anglo-American relations.

Slavery and the African slave trade. Created problems because although both England and the United States had abolished slave trading, the United States did not actively enforce its prohibition.

1841, *Creole* incident. The brig *Creole* sailed from Virginia toward New Orleans with a cargo of slaves, making a legal voyage from one state to another. But the slaves seized the ship and put into the British port of Nassau in the Bahama Islands in the Caribbean. The British, who had abolished slavery in 1834, arrested the ringleaders but freed most of the slaves, despite United States protests.

1842, WEBSTER-ASHBURTON TREATY

Worked out by Secretary of State Daniel Webster and Britain's Alexander Baring, whose title was Lord Ashburton.

Set the present Maine-Canada boundary with the United States giving up 5,000 square miles in northern Maine.

England ceded 6,500 square miles between Lake Superior and Lake of the Woods, which later was found to contain the valuable Mesabi iron deposits.

Agreed to suppress the slave trade by maintaining separate but cooperating naval squadrons off the African coast.

Texas

1530s—Cabeza de Vaca crossed Texas and claimed the area for Spain.

1530s–1821—A colony of Spain.

1821–1836—Part of the Republic of Mexico

1836–1845—Independent Republic of Texas.

1845—Annexed by the United States.

Stephen F. Austin (1793–1836). Received a grant from Mexico to bring American settlers into Texas. They began arriving in 1821. By 1830, some 20,000 had come, bringing their slaves and planting cotton.

Alamo. Colonel William B. Travis led the Texans against General Santa Anna's Mexican army at the Battle of the Alamo in San Antonio. The Mexican army was victorious on March 6, 1836, and all survivors were killed, including Travis, Davy Crockett, and Jim Bowie. The battle marked a low point in the morale of the Texas forces but also provided the rallying cry "Remember the Alamo." Note the picture on p. 349.

Battle of San Jacinto. On April 21, 1836, the Texans scored an outstanding victory over the Mexican army at the San Jacinto River near present-day Houston. The Texans were led by Sam Houston, a former congressman and governor of Tennessee, who later became president of the Republic of Texas.

Manifest Destiny

A term used to describe the spirit of continental expansionism which existed in the United States in the 1840s. The phrase was coined by a journalist named John L. O'Sullivan in July 1845. He warned against foreign powers, namely Great Britain, saying it was "the fulfillment of our manifest destiny to overspread the continent allotted by Providence for the free development of our early multiplying millions."

Oregon

1778—Claimed by Captain James Cook for England.

1792—The American captain Robert Gray sailed up the Columbia River.

1805—Lewis and Clark visited the area.

1818—Joint occupation by England and the United States.

1840s—"Oregon fever" hit, and pioneers trekked over the Oregon Trail to settle the area.

1846—United States and England agreed to divide the territory along the 49th parallel.

Oregon Trail. The route from Independence, Missouri, to the mouth of the Columbia River on the Pacific coast, which was the main highway for pioneers to Oregon. The trail was 2,000 miles long, and it took about five months to make the trip. See the map on p. 352.

Annexation

Annexation of Oregon. Arranged by treaty between Great Britain and the United States in 1846. Some Americans had wanted all the territory and used the slogan "54° 40' or fight." But President Polk agreed on the 49th parallel, following that line from the Rockies to Puget Sound. Britain received Vancouver Island and the right to navigate the Columbia River. Both nations retained free use of the Strait of Juan de Fuca.

Election of 1844. Henry Clay was the Whig candidate and James K. Polk was the Democratic nominee. The Democrats' slogan was the "reannexation of Texas and the reoccupation of Oregon," while Clay and the Whigs hedged on the expansionist policy. There was a third party in the race, the Liberty party, an antislavery group first organized in 1840, whose candidate was James G. Birney. The election was close, but the Democrat Polk won.

1845, Annexation of Texas. Tyler interpreted the election as a mandate for expansion and asked Congress to pass a joint resolution annexing Texas before he left office.

Texas entered the Union as a slave state in December 1845.

As many as four new states could be carved from its territory, but only with its approval.

Texas retained title to all public lands within its boundaries.

Texas accepted full responsibility for debts incurred while an independent republic.

JAMES K. POLK (1795–1849), 11th President

Born in North Carolina; graduated from the University of North Carolina; and practiced law in Tennessee.

Democratic member of the House of Representatives (1825–1839).

Governor of Tennessee (1839–1841).

President (1845–1849).

War with Mexico

John Slidell (1793–1871). Sent to Mexico on a diplomatic mission from December 1845 to March 1846. Mexico owed $2 million in claims to American citizens, and Slidell was authorized to cancel the debt in exchange for Mexico's diplomatically recognizing the annexation of Texas and accepting the Rio Grande River rather than the Nueces River as the southern border. Slidell was also empowered by President Polk to offer $5 million to buy New Mexico and $25 million for California. The Mexican government refused to negotiate with Slidell, and he returned to the United States, convinced that military tactics rather than diplomacy would be necessary.

General Zachary Taylor (1784–1850). Known as "Old Rough and Ready," went to Texas in July 1845 and camped on the Nueces River, near Corpus Christi. After the failure of Slidell's mission in March 1846, he advanced to the Rio Grande and built Fort Texas, later named Fort Brown, across the Rio Grande from the Mexican town of Matamoros. When a Mexican force crossed the river into territory which Mexico also claimed and attacked an American patrol, the United States found the excuse it had been looking for. "War exists," General Taylor wired to President Polk.

PRESIDENT POLK'S THREE-PRONGED DESIGN FOR THE WAR

Clear the Mexicans from Texas and occupy northern Mexico. To accomplish this, General Taylor marched his troops through south Texas and into northern Mexico, culminating in a victory at Buena Vista. Note map "The Mexican War 1846–1848" on p. 359.

Take possession of California and New Mexico. These areas were taken in separate actions by settlers at Sonoma; Captain John C. Frémont at Monterey, California; Commodore John D. Sloat at Monterey and San Francisco; and General Stephen Kearny who took Sante Fe, New Mexico, and then marched to California.

March on Mexico City and force authorities to sign an acceptable peace. General Winfield Scott landed an army at Veracruz, defeated a large Mexican force at Cerro Gordo, spent the summer at Puebla, and then took Mexico City.

General Winfield Scott (1786–1866). Considered the greatest American general between Washington and Lee. Scott fought in the War of 1812, was in Charleston during the nullification crisis (1832), in Maine during the Aroostook War (1839), and became supreme commander of the army in 1841. Scott's personality was somewhat pompous, and he was known as "Old Fuss and Feathers." After the war he was nominated for the presidency by the Whig party in 1852, but was defeated.

Nicholas Trist (1800–1874). Chief clerk of the State Department who was sent to Mexico to accompany Scott's army and act as peace commissioner after the fall of Mexico City. The city fell in September 1847, but because of unstable conditions in the government, Trist could not begin negotiations until January 1848. Meanwhile President Polk, unable to understand the delay, recalled him. Trist ignored the order, negotiated the treaty, and sent it back to Washington with a newspaperman. Furious that Trist had disobeyed orders, Polk accepted the treaty but fired Trist from his State Department job without paying him for his mission. It was not until 1870 that Congress finally awarded Trist his back salary.

1848, TREATY OF GUADALUPE HIDALGO
Mexico ceded New Mexico and Upper California to the United States.
Mexico recognized the Rio Grande River as the southern boundary of Texas.
United States paid Mexico $15 million.
United States assumed claims of American citizens against Mexico which amounted to $3.25 million.

Slavery and the Territories

1846, Wilmot Proviso. A proposed amendment to an appropriations bill for the conduct of the Mexican War and the acquisition of Mexican territory. It was presented by David Wilmot, congressman from Pennsylvania, and stated that slavery should not be permitted in any territory gained from Mexico. The amendment passed the House twice but was defeated in the Senate.

The Proviso was countered by a series of resolutions introduced in the Senate by John C. Calhoun which argued that Congress had no right to bar slavery from any territory. These resolutions had no chance in the northern-dominated House of Representatives. The proposals were significant because they illustrated the growing debate over slavery in the western territories.

Popular sovereignty. An alternative to the question of whether or not slavery should be allowed in the West. The answer was to let the people in the western territories decide for themselves. Senator Lewis Cass of Michigan put forward this idea by calling for the organization of new territories without mentioning slavery.

Compromise of 1850. Five separate bills pushed through Congress by Henry Clay and Stephen Douglas in an attempt to smooth the friction between the sections of the country, particularly with regard to the slavery issue.

1. California entered the Union as a free state. See the map "Free and Slave Areas, 1850" on p. 366.
2. New Mexico and Utah were organized as territories and could enter the Union later with or without slavery, that is, under popular sovereignty.
3. Texas accepted a narrower western boundary in exchange for the United States government giving it $10 million to pay off the $10 million debt left over from its days as a republic.
4. Slave trade, but not slavery, in Washington, D.C., was abolished as of January 1, 1851.

ZACHARY TAYLOR (1784–1850), 12th President

Born in Virginia and grew up in Kentucky.

Joined the army and became an Indian fighter in the Midwest and in Florida.

Became a military hero during the Mexican War as a result of his victories at Monterey and Buena Vista.

President (1849–1850); the last Whig to be elected to the presidency.

Died in office, succeeded by Millard Fillmore.

MILLARD FILLMORE (1800–1874), 13th President

Born in New York and became a self-taught lawyer.

Served one term (1833–1835) in the House of Representatives as a member of the Anti-Masonic party and three times (1837–1843) as a Whig.

Vice-president under Zachary Taylor (1849–1850).

President (1850–1853).

Unsuccessful candidate for president (1856) on the Know-Nothing, or American, ticket.

5. Stricter Fugitive Slave Law was passed in an attempt to end the abolitionist practice of aiding runaway slaves. Federal commissioners were appointed with the authority to pursue runaways and to return them to their owners in the South.

OTHER TERMS TO IDENTIFY

Franklin map. During the peace negotiations in Paris to end the American Revolution, Benjamin Franklin had marked the boundary between Maine and Canada on a map with a heavy red line. The map disappeared, but Daniel Webster, wanting to settle the boundary dispute once again in 1842, simply fabricated a map of the area which he passed off as the original. Webster had someone mark the map along the boundary claimed by the British; then he showed the map to representatives of Massachusetts, which claimed Maine until 1820, so that they would give in to a settlement and thus avoid war. Ironically, the British had a true copy of the Franklin map, which showed that the whole area in dispute rightfully belonged to the United States.

General Stephen Kearny (1794–1848). A military officer who took Santa Fe, New Mexico, with little resistance in August 1846 and then marched with some of his troops to join operations in San Diego and Los Angeles. Note map "The Mexican War" on p. 359.

Barnburners. Name given to radical Democrats in the 1840s, particularly the followers of Martin Van Buren. Conservative Democrats accused them of being willing to burn down their political "barn" in order to get rid of rats, that is, undesirable persons and policies, in the party. Barnburners were especially opposed to the extension of slavery in the territories. In 1848 they joined the Free Soil party to nominate Martin Van Buren for the presidency.

Free Soil party. Political party founded in 1848 and made up of Democratic Barnburners and members of the Liberty party. The name of their party had nothing to do with free land; instead it referred to their desire to prohibit the extension of slavery into the territory acquired in the Mexican War. Free Soil meant free from slavery. The party nominated ex-President Martin Van Buren in 1848, and by the early 1850s it dissolved, many of its members joining the new Republican party.

GLOSSARY

affidavit. A written declaration made under oath before a notary public or other authorized officer. The Fugitive Slave Act which was included in the Compromise of

1850 stated that runaway slaves were to be returned to their owners without jury trial merely upon the submission of an affidavit by the owner. The affidavit would be a sworn statement as to the ownership of the slave.

dark horse. Originally referred to a little known entrant in a horse race. The term has also come to mean a person who receives unexpected support as a candidate for the nomination at a political convention. Often the person is a compromise candidate, as, for example, Polk, who was put forward to break the deadlock between Van Buren and Calhoun.

eyes of Argus. In Greek mythology, Argus was a giant with 100 eyes. One who looks with the eyes of Argus is watchful and alert. Southern congressmen had a tendency to watch over the institution of slavery with the eyes of Argus, ever ready to defend it.

fait accompli. A French term which literally means "an accomplished fact." When General Taylor wrote President Polk about the 1846 skirmish on the Texas border, Polk looked upon the matter as if war already existed, or was a *fait accompli.*

"Fire Bell in the Night." A phrase of Thomas Jefferson's in 1821 in reference to the controversy over the admission of Missouri as a slave state. The dispute, he wrote, "like a fire bell in the night, awakened and filled me with terror." Note the heading on p. 361.

guava. A fruit with a yellow rind and pink flesh used for making jelly or preserves. When Nicholas Trist first arrived in Mexico, he and General Scott did not get along. But when Trist became ill, Scott sent him a jar of guava marmalade, and after that goodwill gesture they became friends.

higher law. The law of God. William Seward used this phrase to refer to a law higher than the Constitution. Because the Constitution and the Fugitive Slave Law legalized the institution of slavery, Seward advocated disobeying them in this regard.

mother lode. A long vein of gold-bearing rock in central California, along the western foothills of the Sierra Nevada. It was first exploited in 1848.

teetotaler. A person who abstains completely from drinking alcoholic beverages. Lewis Cass, who popularized the idea of popular sovereignty, circulated at Washington social functions pretending to drink, even though he was a teetotaler.

WORDS TO KNOW

Define the following, using the dictionary if necessary.

acrimonious   salved
affidavit   sundered
asperities   surfeit
emissary   volubility

SAMPLE QUESTIONS

Matching

1. _____ The secretary of state who negotiated the treaty with England which settled the boundary between Maine and New Brunswick.

2. _____ A former congressman and governor of Tennessee who was elected president of the Republic of Texas in 1836.

3. _____ The president who led the Democrats in demanding that Texas be "reannexed" and Oregon be "reoccupied."

4. _____ American envoy to Mexico who was unsuccessful in his attempt to settle the Texas boundary and to purchase New Mexico and California.

5. _____ American general who captured Santa Fe and southern California during the Mexican War.

6. _____ General during the Mexican War who became president of the United States.

a. Stephen Kearny.
b. James K. Polk.
c. Daniel Webster.
d. Henry Clay.
e. Zachary Taylor.
f. Sam Houston.
g. John Slidell.
h. Nicholas Trist.
i. Lewis Cass.
j. David Wilmot.

7. _____ The Democratic
presidential candidate
in 1848 who called for
"popular sovereignty"
concerning slavery in
the new territories.

8. _____ The State Department
chief clerk who
negotiated the Treaty
of Guadalupe Hidalgo
with Mexico, ignoring
his recall by President
Polk.

9. _____ Congressman from
Pennsylvania who
proposed that slavery
be prohibited from any
territory acquired from
Mexico.

10. _____ The Whig politician
who proposed the
Compromise of 1850.

Multiple Choice

1. Which is the correct chronological order in which the following
   places became parts of the United States?
   a. Texas, Oregon, California.
   b. Oregon, Texas, California.
   c. California, Oregon, Texas.
   d. Oregon, California, Texas.
2. The concept of Manifest Destiny is most closely associated with
   the administration of:
   a. Zachary Taylor.
   b. James K. Polk.
   c. John Tyler.
   d. William Henry Harrison.

3. The Treaty of Guadalupe Hidalgo did all of the following except:
   a. set the boundary of Texas at the Rio Grande River.
   b. cede New Mexico and California to the United States.
   c. pay Mexico $15 million dollars.
   d. make Nicholas Trist a hero after he returned home.
4. According to the doctrine of popular sovereignty, the decision to allow slaves in a territory should be left to the:
   a. president.
   b. Congress.
   c. Supreme Court.
   d. people in the territory.
5. The South won its chief concession in that part of the Compromise of 1850 which concerned:
   a. slavery in New Mexico and Utah.
   b. slavery in the District of Columbia.
   c. fugitive slaves.
   d. the admission of a new state.

ANSWERS
Matching: 1. c 2. f 3. b 4. g 5. a 6. e 7. i 8. h 9. j 10. d
Multiple Choice: a, b, d, d, c

13 / THE SECTIONS GO THEIR WAYS

CHAPTER CHECKLIST

Agriculture

Cotton, tobacco, corn, and wheat. The important crops in the South.

Edmund Ruffin (1794–1865). A Virginia planter who introduced the use of marl, a soil rich in calcium, to counteract the acidity of worn-out tobacco fields. In 1832 he published an *Essay on Calcareous Manures,* and he also edited the *Farmers' Register* (1833–1842). Ruffin's work in soil chemistry led to reforms in farming designed to rejuvenate southern agriculture.

Slavery

Isaac Franklin. An interstate slave trader who made a great deal of money in the 1850s. He and his partner, John Armfield, collected slaves in Alexandria, Virginia, and shipped them to a depot near Natchez. The business was so profitable that the prejudice against slave traders began to disappear. Franklin eventually retired and became a wealthy planter, owning six plantations in Louisiana and one in Tennessee.

Nat Turner. A slave who led a revolt in southern Virginia in 1831. The plot involved about 70 slaves, who killed 57 whites. In the counterattack that followed, 100 slaves were killed, and 20 more were executed following trial. The Nat Turner uprising was significant because the anxiety which it generated among whites led to stricter state laws governing slaves and free blacks alike and a greater southern fear of the propaganda of the abolitionists.

Denmark Vesey. A West Indian slave who bought his freedom and settled in Charleston, South Carolina. For five years he plotted a slave uprising, but at the last minute his plans were betrayed to the authorities. The revelation of the conspiracy in 1822 led to arrests, trials, and 35 executions. It also resulted in the Negro Seaman's Act, intended to prevent the entrance into Charleston of black sailors who might stir up unrest among South Carolina slaves.

Manufacturing

William Gregg. An important textile manufacturer in South Carolina, who established his factory at Graniteville in 1846. Gregg tried to weaken the general southern prejudice against manufacturing and business and established a model community with schools and other facilities for the poor whites whom he hired as workers. By 1850 Gregg employed 300 white textile workers, a large number for the South but small when compared with northern manufacturers.

Industrial expansion. Factories were larger, more specialized, and more mechanized in the second quarter of the 19th century. See the chart "Ten Leading Manufactured Products, 1860" on p. 379.

Inventions were developed and workers quickly adapted to new machines.

New natural resources were discovered, and more raw materials such as cotton and grain were produced as settlement pushed west.

Boilers and steam engines were developed, and steam power began to replace water power.

Immigration increased the labor supply.

New sources of capital appeared as both Europeans and Americans invested in the economy and California gold was added to the supply.

Expanded markets brought about by transportation improvements, population growth, and the relatively high buying power of the people also contributed to the expansion of industry.

Labor

Irish and Germans made up most of the immigrant force, especially
between 1847 and 1854. The Germans often moved into western
farming areas, whereas the Irish remained in urban centers, particularly working in New England mills.

1840. Martin Van Buren granted the 10-hour day to federal employees.

1842. *Commonwealth* v. *Hunt,* a Massachusetts court decision that
established the basic legality of labor unions, but membership in
unions before the Civil War remained small.

Foreign Commerce

Imports and exports. Cotton was the most valuable export; textiles
and iron products were the biggest imports. Most trade was with Great
Britain.

Sailing packet. A boat that follows a regular route, carrying pas-
sengers, freight, and mail. There were 52 packets operating between
New York and various European ports by 1845, and more between New
York and other coastal cities.

Whaling fleets. Prospered between 1830 and 1860 and caused
towns such as New Bedford, Massachusetts, to flourish. Whale oil was
used in lanterns and for fuel.

Clipper ships. Long, fast sailing ships which were built in Boston,
New York, and Baltimore. They cut the sailing time from the Atlantic
seaboard around South America to San Francisco from five or six
months to three, but to achieve such speed, cargo capacity was sacri-
ficed. Note the picture on p. 387.

Steamships. Captured much of the passenger and first-class freight
movement by the late 1840s. Iron ships became more important and
took away the advantage of American shipwrights and their cheap lumber supplies. See the picture on p. 393.

Internal Travel by Water

Mississippi River. Continued to move goods from farm to market,
culminating in New Orleans.

Canals. Became increasingly important in the 1840s, particularly
the Erie Canal, whose volume of western commerce continued to rise.

Railroads

1820s. First built in England, then in the United States.

EARLY PROBLEMS

Different gauges, a gauge being the width between the two rails of the
track. Companies varied the sizes deliberately to prevent other railroads from tying into their tracks.

Engineering problems on curves and slopes.

Fires caused by sparks from wood-burning locomotives.

Weakness of wooden rails topped with strap iron.

IMPROVEMENTS

Engines that burned hard coal.

Iron T-rail which improved the durability of the tracks.

Crossties, that is, wood or metal beams which connected and supported the rails. They were a significant improvement because they
reduced vibration.

1850s. A tremendous burst of railroad construction. See the map
"Railroads, 1850–1861" on p. 389.

Financing Railroads

Private investors. Supplied three-fourths of capital before 1860.
They generally preferred bonds to stocks. A stock is a certificate showing ownership of a portion of a corporation. The commitment can be
short-term, for the stock can be sold at will. A bond is a certificate
showing that a loan has been made to a corporation; no ownership is
involved. The investor making the loan receives interest on his bond.
Both stocks and bonds were sold to raise money for the railroads.

Public aid. Towns, counties, and states loaned money and invested
in stocks. Some states granted exemption from taxation and the right to
condemn property. Condemning property means that a governmental
body forces a private owner to sell property to that body for a public
purpose. Some states actually built and operated railroads as public
corporations. At the national level Congress did little because financial
aid to railroads was usually blocked by a combination of eastern and
southern votes.

"Land-grant" railroads. Railroads which received federal aid in the
form of grants of public land. In 1850 Congress voted to give federal
lands to the states to build a railroad from Lake Michigan to the Gulf of
Mexico. The main beneficiary was the Illinois Central, which received a
200-foot right of way and alternate strips of land along the track one
mile wide and six miles deep. The railroad company received a total of
2.6 million acres and made money by mortgaging the land and selling
portions to farmers. This method of aid was used extensively after the
Civil War when the transcontinental railroad was being constructed.

Construction companies. Railroad capitalists were often more concerned with making money from constructing the lines than from operating them.

Erastus Corning. A railroad president who was also mayor of Albany, New York, and a manufacturer of iron. He accepted no salary as president of the Utica and Schenectady Railroad but found it more profitable to sell the rails and other equipment to the company. Although Corning himself was honest, other railroad officials took personal advantage of similar deals.

OTHER TERMS TO IDENTIFY

Bright Yellow. A new, mild variety of tobacco which was introduced in the early 1850s. It grew best in poor soil and gave a great stimulus to tobacco production.

1851, London Crystal Palace Exhibition. An exhibition of industrial products, inventions, and art objects housed in a huge glass structure. It was similar in concept to a present-day world's fair. The American exhibit so impressed the British that they sent two special commissions to the United States to study manufacturing practices. See the picture on p. 380.

Elias Howe (1819–1867). A mechanic in a Lowell, Massachusetts, textile mill who invented the sewing machine. He received a patent in 1846, and its success made possible the ready-made-clothing industry.

John Deere (1804–1886). A blacksmith in Illinois who in 1839 began manufacturing steel plows rather than the earlier cast-iron models.

Cyrus Hall McCormick (1809–1884). Inventor of the reaper, a machine for harvesting grain, in 1831. In 1848 he located his factory in Chicago, which was to become the transportation center for the farms of the Midwest. The McCormick reaper made possible a vast increase in grain output.

Panic of 1857. A temporary financial and agricultural setback. An over-supply of grain on the world market caused grain prices to decline, which hurt railroads and their expansion, and this lessened the demand for other manufactured products. The economy rallied by 1859 but did not completely recover before the Civil War broke out.

GLOSSARY

bale.   A large, compressed package of some product, such as cotton, which is bound
        together. The usual plantation cotton bale weighed 500 pounds.

barren. A tract of unproductive land, often covered with a scrubby growth of trees. "Poor white trash," a phrase used to describe white members of the lowest income group, scratched out a meager subsistence in the pine barrens of the Appalachian Mountains.

cheek by jowl. Jowl can mean either the cheek or the lower jaw. The term "cheek by jowl" means "side by side" or "right next to each other." In the cities, tenements sprang up cheek by jowl with the expensive homes of the wealthy.

Emerald Isle. The island of Ireland. Many immigrants from the Emerald Isle came to the United States and settled in the large eastern seaports.

Freudian insight. Perception of a situation based on the theories of the Austrian physician Sigmund Freud (1856–1939), developer of psychoanalysis. Freud emphasized the relationship between the subconscious and a person's actions.

manumission. Freeing from slavery, or emancipation. In 1859 in all the South only 3,000 blacks out of a slave population of nearly 4 million were manumitted.

proletarian class. Laborers, who work for a wage, not having enough capital, or money, to go into business for themselves or to invest in someone else's business. Karl Marx (1818–1883), the German philosopher who is considered the founder of modern communism, referred to the working classes as the proletariat.

sell "down the river." The practice of selling slaves from the Upper South to buyers in the Deep South because they brought a higher price. Today the term means "to be exploited," "to be taken advantage of."

status quo. An existing condition or the present state of affairs. The Latin term literally means "state in which." For example, most slaves in the pre-Civil War period did not question the status quo.

steerage. The section of a passenger ship, originally located near the rudder, which was the steering apparatus. It provided the cheapest accommodations for passengers and was often used by immigrants coming to the United States.

trunk line. The main line of a transportation or communication system. The number of trunk lines constructed by the railroads in the 1850s continued to grow, causing a decline in freight and passenger rates.

typhus. A serious disease characterized by severe headache, high fever, and a red rash. Epidemics of typhus often broke out among steerage passengers on ships crossing the Atlantic. For example, on one crossing of the ship *Lark,* 158 of 440 passengers died of typhus.

Upper South. The northern states of the South, such as Virginia, Maryland, and North Carolina. Tennessee and Kentucky are sometimes considered border states of the Upper South.

windrow. A long row of cut hay or grain left to dry in a field before being bundled. McCormick's reaper deposited cut grain neatly on a platform from which a man could rake it easily into windrows.

WORDS TO KNOW

Define the following, using the dictionary if necessary.

congenitally	perforce
demise	precipitous
ineptitude	proliferation
paucity	vulcanization

SAMPLE QUESTIONS

Matching

1. _____ Slave trader.

2. _____ Planned an abortive slave revolt in Charleston.

3. _____ Invented sewing machine.

4. _____ Textile manufacturer.

5. _____ Introduced marl to help tobacco fields.

6. _____ Developed the steel plow.

7. _____ Led slave insurrection in Virginia.

8. _____ Manufactured reapers in Chicago.

9. _____ Famous for whaling fleets.

10. _____ Railroad manager.

a. Edmund Ruffin.
b. Isaac Franklin.
c. Nat Turner.
d. Denmark Vesey.
e. William Gregg.
f. New Bedford.
g. Erastus Corning.
h. John Deere.
i. Elias Howe.
j. Cyrus McCormick.

Multiple Choice

1. In general, southern states encouraged free blacks:
   a. to emigrate from the area.
   b. to immigrate into the area.
   c. to live in communes.
   d. to buy the freedom of other slaves.
2. In 1860 the leading manufactured product in the United States was:
   a. flour.
   b. machinery.
   c. cotton textiles.
   d. iron.

3. The most valuable export from the United States before the Civil War was:
   a. iron.
   b. tobacco.
   c. cotton.
   d. rice.
4. Labor unions remained small because of all the following reasons except:
   a. the number of job-hungry immigrants.
   b. the employment of women and children in unskilled jobs.
   c. the assumption that anyone willing to work could eventually escape the wage-earning class.
   d. medical and pension benefits provided to keep workers satisfied.
5. The capitalists who invested in railroads generally made a profit from:
   a. owning mines at the end of the line.
   b. constructing the line.
   c. operating the line.
   d. leasing the line to the government.

ANSWERS
Matching: 1. b 2. d 3. i 4. e 5. a 6. h 7. c 8. j 9. f 10. g
Multiple Choice: a, a, c, d, b

14 / THE COMING OF THE CIVIL WAR

CHAPTER CHECKLIST

Steps Leading to War

Uncle Tom's Cabin. Harriet Beecher Stowe's novel, which heightened antislavery sentiment around the world. Mrs. Stowe began writing it while debate raged over the Fugitive Slave Act of 1850, and it first appeared in serial form in the *National Era,* an antislavery periodical, from June 1851, to April 1852. The book was also successfully adapted as a play, and the characters of the slaves Uncle Tom and Eliza, the white child Eva, and the slave driver Simon Legree became well known.

"Young America" movement. An expansionist feeling which attempted to project the spirit of manifest destiny south to Latin America, west into the Pacific Islands, and north to Canada. This climate of opinion was evident in the late 1840s and 1850s, and exhibited itself in a desire to spread American democracy to other areas.

1854, Ostend Manifesto. A secret report on Cuba prepared in Ostend, Belgium, by three American diplomats in Europe: James Buchanan, minister to Great Britain; John Mason, minister to France; and

Pierre Soulé, minister to Spain. The report was sent to Secretary of State William Marcy and outlined the rationale for buying or, if necessary, taking the island of Cuba from Spain. The news leaked out, and northerners were convinced it was a southern plot to acquire another slave state. The publicity wrecked any hope of obtaining Cuba.

FRANKLIN PIERCE (1804–1869), 14th President

Born in New Hampshire; graduated from Bowdoin; and
    practiced law.
Democratic member of the House of Representatives
    (1833–1837).
United States senator (1837–1842).
President (1853–1857).

1853, Gadsden Purchase. A treaty with Mexico negotiated by the United States minister James Gadsden. For $10 million the United States acquired land in present-day New Mexico and Arizona which included an easy route over the mountains for a railroad. This purchase made possible a southern route for the proposed transcontinental railroad. See the painting on p. 403.

1854, Kansas-Nebraska Act. Legislation sponsored by Senator Stephen Douglas which officially created the Nebraska Territory and the Kansas Territory. In addition, it repealed the 1820 Missouri Compromise and stated that popular sovereignty would determine the future of slavery in those two areas, rather than the previous dividing line of 36° 30′. The act reopened the issue of the extension of slavery into the territories and caused further difficulties between the North and the South.

NEW POLITICAL PARTIES
Know-Nothing party. Also known as the American party, active between 1853 and 1856. It was anti-Roman Catholic and anti-immigrant. The party got its name because originally it was a secret organization for Protestants whose password was "I don't know." Calling themselves the American party in 1856, they ran Millard Fillmore for president. By this time, however, the party was split over the slavery issue, and many northern supporters joined the Republicans.
Republican party. Started in 1854, composed of former Free Soilers, Conscience Whigs (the Whigs who opposed slavery), "Anti-Nebraska" Democrats (opposed the Kansas-Nebraska Act), and

northern members of the Know-Nothings. The one major demand of the party was that slavery be kept out of the territories, but they did not propose abolishing it where it already was. This party, started in the 1850s, is the same Republican party in existence today. It should not be confused with Jefferson's Democratic Republican party, which is today's Democratic party.

Bleeding Kansas. A term referring to the violence in the Kansas Territory as proslavery and antislavery forces tried to take hold in the area after it was opened as a territory in 1854. See the map "Bleeding Kansas" on p. 405.

1856, Caning of Charles Sumner (1811–1874). An event which illustrated the emotional response of southerners to abolitionists. Charles Sumner, senator from Massachusetts from 1851 to 1874, made an impassioned speech in the Senate against the Kansas situation and slavery in general, and in the speech he made insulting remarks about a southern colleague and slaveowner, Senator Andrew Butler of South Carolina, who was not present. Two days later Butler's nephew, Preston Brooks, a member of the House of Representatives from South Carolina, marched over to the Senate to redeem the family honor. Brooks waited until the Senate adjourned and then went down to Sumner, still writing at his desk, and beat him with his walking cane. Primarily because of psychological damage, Sumner was unable to return to the Senate for three years. Brooks was officially censured, or reprimanded, by the House of Representatives for his actions, so he resigned his seat and was then triumphantly reelected by his South Carolina constituents. Note the drawing on p. 407.

JAMES BUCHANAN (1791–1868), 15th President

Born in Pennsylvania; graduated from Dickinson; and practiced law.

Began his political career as a Federalist but switched to the Democratic party in the 1820s.

Member of the House of Representatives (1821–1831).

Minister to Russia (1832–1833).

United States senator (1834–1845).

Secretary of state under President Polk (1845–1849).

Minister to Great Britain (1853–1856).

President (1857–1861).

1857, Dred Scott decision. The Supreme Court stated that Congress could not deny a person the right to take his property, including slaves, into any territory he wished. Dred Scott was a slave who was taken by his master, an army surgeon, from Missouri, a slave state, into Illinois, a free state, and then Wisconsin, a territory declared free under the Missouri Compromise. Scott then returned to Missouri, and after his master died, he sued for freedom on the grounds that residency in free areas had made him free. Scott's emancipation was not really in question because his master's widow had married an abolitionist, and Scott was to be freed no matter what the outcome. The Supreme Court, presided over by Chief Justice Roger Taney, made several pronouncements in this decision. First, it was declared that a slave was not a citizen and therefore could not sue in a federal court. Furthermore, under the Constitution, the government could not deprive a person of life, liberty, or property without due process of law, and therefore the 1820 Missouri Compromise, even before it had been repealed by the 1854 Kansas-Nebraska Act, had been unconstitutional. In summary, the Dred Scott decision declared a law of Congress unconstitutional for the first time since *Marbury* v. *Madison* (1803). It also stated that slavery could not be excluded from federal territories.

1856, Lecompton Constitution. A proslavery document drawn up at a constitutional convention in Lecompton, Kansas. The free-soil forces refused to participate in the election of delegates to this convention. President Buchanan encouraged Congress to accept the proposed state constitution and to admit Kansas as a slave state, but the opposition, led by Stephen Douglas, was able to prevent it. Two separate referendums were held in Kansas in 1858 to decide whether or not to accept the Lecompton Constitution. In both cases, the document was rejected. Kansas finally entered the Union in 1861 as a free state.

1858, Lincoln-Douglas debates. Held in Illinois where the Republican, Abraham Lincoln, and the Democrat, Stephen Douglas, were competing for a seat in the United States Senate. Since senators were elected by the state legislatures until the Seventeenth Amendment passed in 1913, the two men were not appealing directly to the people for votes but were asking them to elect certain state legislators who would in turn vote for them for senator. One major issue was whether or not slavery should be excluded from the territories. Douglas won the election but Lincoln won national recognition as a spokesman for Republican principles.

  Freeport Doctrine. A point made by Douglas at the debate held in
    Freeport, Illinois, which illustrated his continued support for popu-
    lar sovereignty. Lincoln asked Douglas if, considering the Dred
    Scott decision, a territory could exclude slavery. The Supreme
    Court had said it could not, but Douglas replied that if local police

officials did not enforce slavery regulations, then the institution would not exist. In other words, it would be difficult for slavery to exist in an area where the local populace did not want it. This pronouncement hurt Douglas two years later when he was the Democratic presidential candidate because southern Democrats refused to accept a man who said the Dred Scott decision could be circumvented.

1859, John Brown's raid. An attack on a United States arsenal at Harpers Ferry, Virginia, led by John Brown, an ardent abolitionist who was mentally unbalanced. With 16 white and 5 black men he made his raid, planning to distribute the weapons captured to local slaves who would join the uprising. Brown was tried and hanged, and he became a martyr to northern abolitionists. Note the painting on p. 415.

Election of 1860. Lincoln won the election in which four parties nominated candidates. Note the map entitled "The Election of 1860" on p. 417.

Republican. Lincoln led the Republicans in opposing the extension of slavery into the territories.

Democratic (Northern). Stephen Douglas got the support of the northern Democrats, but his Freeport Doctrine caused southerners to bolt the party.

Democratic (Southern). John C. Breckinridge of Kentucky, the nominee of the southern Democrats, declared that citizens could take their "property" into any territory.

Constitutional Union. John Bell of Tennessee led those remnants of Whigs and Know-Nothings who tried to ignore the slavery issue.

December 20, 1860. A special convention called by the South Carolina legislature voted to secede from the Union. Within six weeks they were joined by the other states of the Lower South.

February 1861. In Montgomery, Alabama, a provisional government of the Confederate States of America was established. It was later moved to Richmond. Jefferson Davis was elected president.

OTHER TERMS TO IDENTIFY

Personal liberty laws. Legislation passed by northern states to keep the Fugitive Slave Act (1850) from being enforced. The Massachusetts Personal Liberty Act (1855) made a state officer subject to fines and imprisonment for arresting a suspected runaway slave.

William Walker (1824–1860). An American filibuster who seized control of Nicaragua and made himself president for two years from 1855 to 1857. There were even rumors concerning communication with

President Pierce about the admission of Nicaragua as a slave state. In 1860, while trying to recapture part of Central America, Walker was captured and shot in Honduras.

"General" George W. L. Bickley. An adventurer who tried to organize an expedition into northern Mexico. He attempted to get the support of proslavery factions by suggesting that Mexico be divided into no less than 25 slave states.

1850, Clayton-Bulwer Treaty. Negotiated by Secretary of State John Clayton and the British minister Sir Henry Bulwer, the treaty provided that any future canal built across Central America would be jointly controlled by the two countries. This treaty governed Anglo-American relations in the area until the 1901 Hay-Pauncefote Treaty, which gave the United States the right to construct and own such a canal by herself.

Matthew Perry (1794–1858). Naval officer who negotiated a treaty with Japan (1854) permitting the United States to open a consulate and to use certain Japanese ports. See the picture on p. 400. Commodore Perry was the younger brother of Oliver Hazard Perry, a naval hero in the War of 1812.

Stephen Douglas (1813–1861). Democratic Illinois senator, known as the "Little Giant," who was an advocate of popular sovereignty in the territories. He helped steer the Compromise of 1850 and sponsored the Kansas-Nebraska Act of 1854. In 1860 he was the presidential candidate for the northern wing of the Democratic party. Douglas died suddenly from typhoid fever in 1861. See his picture on p. 401.

New England Emigrant Aid Society. An organization formed in 1854 to help antislavery settlers move to Kansas. Their goal was to assure that when the time came for voting under popular sovereignty to decide whether Kansas would enter the Union as a free or a slave state, the area would have a majority of antislavery forces.

Border Ruffians. Men from Missouri who crossed the border into Kansas to vote illegally, primarily for proslavery candidates. In 1854 they were partially responsible for electing a proslavery territorial delegate to Congress, and in 1855 the Border Ruffians helped elect a proslavery territorial legislature.

John C. Frémont (1813–1890). An explorer known as "the Path-finder" and a hero of the conquest of California during the Mexican War. Frémont was the first Republican candidate for president in 1856, and the party slogan that year was "Free soil, free speech, and Frémont." "Frémont lost to the Democrat, James Buchanan.

1861, Crittenden Compromise. A constitutional amendment proposed by Senator John J. Crittenden of Kentucky and a group of moderates. They proposed that slavery be authorized in all territories south of latitude 36° 30', the old Missouri Compromise line, and that no future amendment would tamper with the institution of slavery where it already existed. Lincoln and his Republican supporters refused to consider opening any new territory to slavery, and the attempted compromise died.

GLOSSARY

Capitol.   The building in Washington, D.C., which houses the Congress of the United States. The *capital* is the town or city that is the official seat of government in a state or nation.

crepe.   A fabric which, worn or displayed in black, is a sign of mourning. When Anthony Burns, a runaway slave from Virginia, was arrested in Boston, a sympathetic mob tried to free him. The federal commissioner finally ruled that he must be returned to his master, and as he and a military escort marched to the dock to board a ship, buildings all along the route were festooned, or draped, with black crepe as a sign of mourning for returning the fugitive slave.

guttapercha cane.   A walking stick made from the latex of a guttapercha tree, a tropical tree most commonly found in Malaysia. The texture of the substance resembles rubber.

Lower South.   A term used to refer to the states of South Carolina, Georgia, Florida, Alabama, Mississippi, Louisiana, and Texas. The states of the Lower South had seceded by February 1, 1861. The term Deep South is even more limited and usually refers to South Carolina, Georgia, Alabama, and Mississippi.

wheelhorse.   A steady, dependable worker, especially in a political organization. Abraham Lincoln was a party wheelhorse, first as a Whig, then as a Republican. In a team of horses, the wheelhorse is the horse that follows the leader and is harnessed nearest to the front wheels.

WORDS TO KNOW

Define the following, using the dictionary if necessary.

cacophony	megalomaniac
exacerbated	moribund
freebooter	pique
importuned	punctilio

SAMPLE QUESTIONS

Matching

1. _____ American adventurer who made himself president of Nicaragua for two years.

2. _____ Secretary of state who negotiated a treaty for joint Anglo-American control of any canal constructed across Central America.

3. _____ Naval officer who went to Japan in 1852 to try to open trade with that country.

4. _____ Democratic senator from Illinois who introduced the Kansas-Nebraska Act in 1854 and ran for president in 1860.

5. _____ Abolitionist who led an attack on Pottawatomie Creek, Kansas, in 1856 and on Harpers Ferry, Virginia, in 1859.

6. _____ Whig president who later ran on the Know-Nothing ticket.

7. _____ Democratic president who asked Congress, without success, to admit Kansas into the Union under the pro-slavery Lecompton constitution.

a. John Brown.
b. Roger Taney.
c. James Buchanan.
d. Franklin Pierce.
e. Stephen Douglas.
f. Millard Fillmore.
g. Matthew Perry.
h. William Walker.
i. John Crittenden.
j. John Clayton.

8. _____ Winner of the 1852 presidential election.

9. _____ Chief Justice of the Supreme Court.

10. _____ Kentucky senator who proposed a constitutional amendment which would guarantee slavery in all territory south of latitude 36° 30'.

Multiple Choice

1. The Ostend Manifesto concerned the possible annexation of:
   a. Hawaii.
   b. Cuba.
   c. Nicaragua.
   d. Mexico.
2. The status of slavery in the territory of the Louisiana Purchase was not affected by the:
   a. Dred Scott decision.
   b. Kansas-Nebraska Act.
   c. Compromise of 1850.
   d. Missouri Compromise.
3. Which was a provision of the Kansas-Nebraska Act?
   a. Kansas was declared a free state.
   b. The Dred Scott decision was nullified.
   c. Popular sovereignty was provided for in these two territories.
   d. The 36° 30' line was extended to the Pacific.
4. The original platform of the Republican party was:
   a. abolition of slavery.
   b. popular sovereignty in the territories.
   c. no expansion of slavery into the territories.
   d. to ignore the issue of slavery.
5. What was the principle established by the Dred Scott decision?
   a. Congress could abolish slavery in the territories at will.
   b. Slaves residing in a free state automatically became free.

    c. Slavery was a national institution, excluded only where state governments abolished it.

    d. Through popular sovereignty, the territories had the sole right to determine the status of slavery.

15 / THE WAR TO SAVE THE UNION

CHAPTER CHECKLIST

Jefferson Davis (1808–1889)

Born in Kentucky; grew up in Mississippi; educated at West Point.
Democratic member of the House of Representatives (1845–1846) and of the Senate (1847–1851).
Secretary of War under President Pierce (1853–1857).
President of the Confederate States of America (1861–1865).
Imprisoned for two years after the Civil War but was released without being tried for treason. See his portrait on p. 427.

ABRAHAM LINCOLN (1809–1865), 16th President

Born in Kentucky and grew up in Indiana and Illinois.
Practiced law and served in the Illinois legislature (1834–1841).
Whig member of the House of Representatives (1847–1849).
Ran for the United States Senate in 1858 as a Republican;
  defeated by Stephen Douglas.
President (1861–1865).
Assassinated on April 12, 1865, by John Wilkes Booth in
  Washington, D.C.

The Union Splits

December 20, 1860. South Carolina seceded from the Union and was soon followed by Mississippi (January 9, 1861), Florida (January 10), Alabama (January 11), Georgia (January 19), Louisiana (January 26), and Texas (February 1).

April 12, 1861. First shots of the war fired at Fort Sumter, South Carolina. Lincoln issued a call for volunteers.

April–May 1861. Other states seceded: Virginia (April 17), Arkansas (May 6), Tennessee (May 7), and North Carolina (May 20).

ADVANTAGES OF EACH SIDE

North had seven times as much manufacturing and a far larger and more efficient railroad system. The North also controlled the merchant marine and the navy with which to blockade the southern states. Furthermore, it had a larger population.

South thought Europe needed southern cotton and predicted, incorrectly, that European countries, particularly Great Britain, would come to her aid. The South fought a defensive war, which was cheaper in terms of men and material and maintained morale. Southerners fought to defend their homes as well as to protect the institution of slavery. Most important, the South had superior military leadership.

Outstanding Generals

NORTH

Ulysses Simpson Grant (1822–1885). A West Point graduate who fought in the Mexican War and resigned from the Army in 1854. He held a series of jobs and had bouts with alcoholism. When the Civil War broke out, he reenlisted and quickly rose in rank. His most important victories were at Vicksburg and at Appomattox. Grant later became the Republican president from 1869 to 1877. See his picture on p. 444.

George McClellan (1826–1885). A West Point graduate who became general in chief of the Army in 1861, was removed from that position the following year, and was reinstated and removed once again, all in 1862. Lincoln's chief complaint against McClellan was that he dallied rather than pursuing the enemy. He was the unsuccessful Democratic candidate for president in 1864, and after the war he pursued an engineering career and served as governor of New Jersey (1878–1881).

William Tecumseh Sherman (1820–1891). Like Grant and McClellan, a West Point graduate who resigned from the Army in the 1850s and reenlisted at the beginning of the Civil War. His most famous campaign was in Georgia in 1864 and is referred to as Sherman's "march to the sea." Sherman is sometimes called "the first modern soldier" because he believed in total war, that is, in appropriating or destroying everything that might help the enemy continue the fight. After the war, Sherman served as general in chief of the Army for 14 years.

SOUTH

Robert Edward Lee (1807–1870). A Virginian who graduated from West Point and followed a military career. In 1862, he became commander of Confederate forces and is generally considered the best overall strategist of the war. In 1865, Lee surrendered his Army of Northern Virginia to Grant at Appomattox Court House. After the war he became president of Washington College in Virginia, now called Washington and Lee University. See Lee's picture on p. 436.

Thomas J. (Stonewall) Jackson (1824–1863). A Virginian, educated at West Point, who served six years in the army and then resigned to teach. As a general for the Confederacy, he won his nickname at the First Battle of Bull Run in 1861, when a fellow officer trying to rally his own men shouted, "Look, there is Jackson with his Virginians, standing like a stone wall against the enemy." Jackson was particularly noted for the swift striking capacity of his troops. His last battle was at Chancellorsville in 1863 where he was accidentally shot and killed by his own troops.

Major Battles

1861, Fort Sumter, South Carolina. The first shots of the war were fired on this Union fortress on an island in Charleston harbor. By April the Union troops there needed food, and Lincoln ordered supply ships to go to the island. The Confederates opened fire before the ships arrived, and the next day the fort fell into southern hands.

July 1861, Bull Run, Virginia. A battle fought on a branch of the Potomac River called Bull Run, which the Confederates won. It is also called the Battle of Manassas, after a nearby town. General McDowell was the Union commander, and General Beauregard led the Confederate troops. As a result of this battle, the Union troops retreated in panic to Washington, D.C., 20 miles away, and many people thought the capital would fall next. See the sketch on p. 429.

There was a Second Battle of Bull Run in August 1862, in which Lee's army was victorious over the Union troops led by General John Pope.

April 1862, Shiloh, Tennessee. A Union victory led by General Grant over the Confederate forces of General Albert Sidney Johnston. Shiloh was a country church 20 miles north of Corinth, Mississippi. Johnston led a surprise attack on Grant's troops and was successful until fresh Union troops were brought in and the southerners fell back. But Grant had been caught off guard and was temporarily relieved of his command. Note the map "War in the West, 1862–1863" on p. 435.

September 1862, Antietam Creek, Maryland. A battle at Sharpsburg led by General McClellan against the Confederate troops of General Lee. Lee had hoped for a victory in a non-Confederate state, but he was outnumbered and his troops were able to slip back into Virginia only because McClellan did not aggressively pursue his advantage. As a result of the Battle of Antietam, Lincoln dismissed McClellan from his command. Note the map "War in the East, 1861–1863" on p. 428.

July 1863, Gettysburg, Pennsylvania. The turning point in the Civil War where General Lee's troops were clearly defeated on the battlefield by the Union forces under General George Meade. However, Meade did not continue his attack, and Lee's army retreated to safety in Virginia. Note the map "Gettysburg Campaign, 1863" on p. 428.

May–July 1863, Vicksburg, Mississippi. General Grant placed the city, defended by General John C. Pemberton, under siege and starved it into submission. The city was important because of its commanding position on the Mississippi River. With Vicksburg in Union hands, federal gunboats could range up and down on the river, and Arkansas and Texas, the breadbasket of the Confederacy, were isolated. Note the map "Vicksburg Campaign, 1863" on p. 435.

September–December 1864, march through Georgia. General Sherman took Atlanta and then marched his army to the port of Savannah. The troops were permitted to live off the land, and as they marched, they denuded a strip of Georgia 60 miles wide. The march had a military objective—to conquer territory; an economic objective—to destroy southern resources; and a psychological objective—to break the South's will to fight as it watched a Union army marching through the Confederacy. Note the map "The War Moves South, 1863–1865" on p. 449.

April 3, 1865, Richmond, Virginia. The Confederate capital fell to Grant's army.

April 9, 1865, Appomattox Court House, Virginia. General Lee surrendered his army to General Grant at a prearranged ceremony in a house in this village. The requirement was that the Confederate soldiers lay down their arms and they could return to their homes in peace. They were also allowed to retain possession of their horses. See the map "War Ends in Virginia, 1864–1865" on p. 447.

Important Acts During the War

Conscription. When the number of volunteers began to slacken, both sides instituted a draft. See the graph "Men Present for Service in the Civil War" on p. 426.

South, 1862, Conscription Act. The draft act passed by the Confederate Congress. It allowed the hiring of substitutes and exempted many classes of people, including college professors and mail carriers. There was also a provision deferring the owners of 20 or more slaves.

North, 1863, Conscription Act. Applied to all men between 20 and 45, but it allowed draftees to hire substitutes and even to buy exemption for $300. Many workingmen resented this discrimination against the poor, and draft riots broke out in various parts of the nation, the most serious occurring in New York City.

1862, Emancipation Proclamation. Issued by Lincoln on September 22 to go into effect on January 1, 1863. It stated that all slaves in areas of rebellion on that date would be free. The Proclamation did not apply to the border states or to areas of the South which had already been captured by federal troops. However, as Union troops moved into new areas of the Confederacy, those slaves would be freed. Actually, all slaves were not freed until the ratification of the Thirteenth Amendment to the Constitution in 1865. See drawings on p. 440.

1862, Homestead Act. Gave 160 acres of public land to any settler who would farm the land for five years.

1862, Morrill Land Grant Act. Gave the states land at the rate of 30,000 acres for each representative and senator from that state to support agricultural colleges. Some states gave the land to existing schools, while others founded new institutions. About 70 new colleges were started as a result.

1862, Pacific Railway Act. Authorized subsidies in land and money for the construction of a transcontinental railroad, which was completed in 1869. This act had been delayed for a decade as the North and South fought over the route. With the southern states no longer represented in Congress, the selection of a route was more easily made.

1863, National Banking Act. Banks would obtain federal charters by investing at least one-third of their capital in United States bonds and then issuing currency up to 90 percent of the value of these bonds. In addition, a 10 percent tax was placed on state bank notes issued. This act eventually drove the state notes out of circulation and established a uniform national currency as we have today.

Results of the War

Black slavery was dead.

The Union could not be dissolved; secession was not possible.

A republican form of government could survive, despite the dissatisfaction of a minority.

Inventions, technical advancements, and a better organized, more productive economic system had emerged.

OTHER TERMS TO IDENTIFY

Blue and gray. The colors of the respective uniforms during the Civil War. Union troops wore blue; Confederate troops gray.

Copperheads. Peace Democrats who opposed all measures in support of the war and wanted to force a negotiated peace.

Alexander Stephens (1812–1883). Vice-president of the Confederacy who often disagreed with the policies of President Jefferson Davis. At one point he even urged his native Georgia to secede from the Confederacy. Stephens served in the House of Representatives from 1843 to 1859 and again after the war, 1873–1882.

***Monitor* vs. *Merrimack*.** A naval battle fought near Virginia on March 9, 1862, between the Union's *Monitor* and the Confederacy's *Merrimack*. It was the first fight in history between armored warships as opposed to wooden ones, and the *Monitor* won.

Bureau of Colored Troops. A governmental agency set up in 1863 to supervise the enlistment of blacks, who had been officially, at least, barred from the Army by a law of 1792. The troops were segregated (and remained so until after World War II) and commanded by white officers. They were paid one-half of the salary of their white counterparts. By 1865 one Union soldier in eight was black.

General Ambrose Burnside (1824–1881). A Union general who was commander of the Army of the Potomac for a brief period in 1863. He replaced General McClellan and was replaced by General Joseph Hooker after Lee's army defeated his forces at Fredericksburg. Burnside was famous for his side whiskers, a type which have since been called "sideburns."

National Union ticket. The combined party of Republicans and War Democrats in the campaign of 1864. Abraham Lincoln, a Republican, was renominated. The vice-presidential candidate was Andrew Johnson of Tennessee, a Democratic senator who had remained in Washington, D.C., rather than secede with his state.

GLOSSARY

breastworks. Temporary, quickly constructed fortifications, usually breast-high. At the siege of Petersburg, Virginia, in 1864, both armies constructed complicated lines of breastworks and trenches, running for miles in a great arc.

Celt. A term sometimes used to refer to the Irish. The feeling against the Irish after they participated so vigorously in the 1863 New York draft riots could be seen in an article in the *Atlantic Monthly* which stated, "It is impossible to name any standard . . . that will give a vote to the Celt and exclude the negro." Originally the term Celt referred to an ancient tribe which lived in central and western Europe from around 2,000 B.C. to 400 B.C. and spread its culture throughout the area, including the British Isles.

coup de grâce. A French term which literally means "a stroke of mercy." It means a finishing or decisive stroke, as to someone who is mortally wounded. After the battle of Shiloh in 1862, the victorious General Grant was still too shaken by General Johnston's unexpected attack and too appalled by the Union's huge losses to apply the *coup de grâce* that might have ended Confederate resistance in the West.

greenbacks. Paper money issued by the Union during the Civil War which could not be turned in, or redeemed, for an equal amount of coin. It was simply printing-press money, not backed by gold in the treasury.

martial law. Temporary rule by military authorities imposed upon a civilian population in time of war. During the Civil War, Lincoln did not hesitate to impose martial law on conquered areas.

matériel. The equipment and supplies, such as guns and ammunition, of a military force. Do not confuse the word with *material.*

pontoon bridges. Temporary floating bridges using pontoons for support. A pontoon is a flat-bottomed boat or other portable float. See the picture on p. 433. To occupy Fredericksburg, Virginia, General Burnside's divisions crossed the Rappahannock River over pontoon bridges.

Victorian standards. Characteristics of the period of Queen Victoria, ruler of the British Empire from 1837 to 1901. There was particular emphasis on being morally straitlaced, at least on the surface, with a stuffy, almost pompous air. Topics pertaining to sex were taboo in "polite society." Some of Lincoln's metaphors, or figures of speech, were considered slightly risqué, or naughty, according to the Victorian standards of the day.

war of attrition. A constant wearing down of the resources of the enemy. In 1864–1865 in Virginia, General Grant fought a slow and grinding war of attrition, never giving Lee's army a chance to catch its breath, to increase its numbers, or to resupply.

West Point. A military reservation in New York which was the site of a Revolutionary fort guarding the Hudson River. In 1802 it became the location of the United States Military Academy, a college to train the country's military leaders. The Civil War generals on both sides had been educated at West Point. Other service academies have since been founded, such as the United States Naval Academy at Annapolis (1845) and the United States Air Force Academy at Colorado Springs (1954).

writ of habeas corpus. A document which states that a person is to be brought before a court or judge, so that the person may be released if held unlawfully. During the Civil War, Lincoln exceeded the usual bounds of presidential power by suspending the writ of habeas corpus in critical areas so that people could be held indefinitely.

Zouave. A member of a French infantry unit, originally composed of recruits from the French colony of Algeria in Africa. *Zouave* was the French adaptation of *Zwawa,* an Algerian tribal name. The group was known for its brightly colored and exotic-looking uniforms and precision drilling. During the Civil War, there were militia companies on both sides which adopted the name, such as the "Louisiana Zouaves."

OFFICERS IN THE MILITARY

ARMY	NAVY
General	Admiral
Lieutenant General	Vice Admiral
Major General	Rear Admiral
Brigadier General	Commodore
Colonel	Captain
Lieutenant Colonel	Commander
Major	Lieutenant Commander
Captain	Lieutenant
First Lieutenant	Lieutenant (junior grade)
Second Lieutenant	Ensign

WORDS TO KNOW

Define the following, using the dictionary if necessary.

audacious	penchant
disapprobation	preponderant
logistical	vise
obtuse	vitriolic

SAMPLE QUESTIONS

Multiple Choice

1. Which was *not* an advantage possessed by the North over the South at the outset of the Civil War?
   a. a superior transportation system.
   b. larger navy and merchant marine.
   c. superior military leadership.
   d. diversified industrial development.
2. The South hoped for England's aid in the Civil War chiefly because of England's:
   a. defense of slavery in her own colonies.
   b. resentment against the United States government's action in the Oregon question.
   c. sympathy with the South on grounds of religion.
   d. need for cotton.
3. During the Civil War, blacks were:
   a. integrated into Union troops.
   b. only allowed to serve as paramedics.
   c. segregated into their own units.
   d. were not allowed to fight.
4. Which of the following abolished slavery in the states of Delaware and Kentucky?
   a. Missouri Compromise.
   b. Emancipation Proclamation.
   c. Thirteenth Amendment.
   d. Wilmot Proviso.
5. Numerous state colleges were founded as a result of land given to the states under the:
   a. Homestead Act.
   b. Morrill Land Grant Act.

    c. National Banking Act.
    d. Pacific Railway Act.

Answer the following by placing a check under Union or Confederacy.

A. CHECK THE SIDE WHICH WON THE FOLLOWING BATTLES:

	UNION	CONFEDERACY
1. Fort Sumter	_____	_____
2. Bull Run	_____	_____
3. *Monitor* vs. *Merrimack*	_____	_____
4. Gettysburg	_____	_____
5. Vicksburg	_____	_____

B. CHECK THE SIDE WHICH THE FOLLOWING INDIVIDUALS
SUPPORTED:

1. Stonewall Jackson	_____	_____
2. George McClellan	_____	_____
3. Alexander Stephens	_____	_____
4. William Sherman	_____	_____
5. Samuel Chase	_____	_____
6. Ambrose Burnside	_____	_____
7. Joseph Johnston	_____	_____
8. Thaddeus Stevens	_____	_____
9. Jefferson Davis	_____	_____
10. William Seward	_____	_____

ANSWERS
Multiple Choice: c, d, c, c, b. (A) Union Victories: 3, 4, 5; (B) Union Leaders: 2, 4, 5, 6, 8, 10.

16 / RECONSTRUCTION AND THE SOUTH

CHAPTER CHECKLIST

Reconstruction. The post-Civil War period, from approximately 1865 to 1877, during which the United States confronted the problems of readmitting the southern states to the Union and integrating the freed slaves into society.

Readmission of the States

Controversies. Should the southern states be readmitted automatically or should conditions be placed on their admission? If conditions were set, who should determine them, the president or Congress?

1863, Lincoln's ten percent plan. A program for reconstruction designed by Lincoln and based on his presidential pardoning power. All southerners with the exception of high Confederate officials and a few other groups could reinstate themselves as United States citizens by taking a loyalty oath. When a number equal to 10 percent of those voting in the 1860 election in a particular state had taken the oath, then that state could set up a state government. The only requirements

152

placed on the new governments were that they be republican, that is, representative; that they must recognize the free status of all blacks; and that they provide for the education of blacks. State governments in Tennessee, Louisiana, and Arkansas were set up under the ten percent plan, which was very much disliked by the Radical Republicans in Congress.

1864, Wade-Davis bill. Passed by both houses of Congress, this bill would have made readmission difficult. It was disposed of by Lincoln with a pocket veto. It required that a majority, rather than 10 percent of the voters, take a loyalty oath to the Union. Those who had been officials in the Confederate government or had voluntarily fought against the United States were barred from voting in the election or serving in the subsequent state constitutional convention. The requirements for the new constitutions were that they prohibit slavery and repudiate all Confederate debts. This unsuccessful bill was favored by the Radical Republicans.

1865, Thirteenth Amendment. Constitutional change which abolished slavery within the United States. An amendment requires a two-thirds vote in both houses of Congress and ratification by three-quarters of the states.

1867, First Reconstruction Act. The southern states excluding Tennessee were divided into five military districts, each controlled by a major general with almost dictatorial power. In order to end military rule and be readmitted to the Union, the states were to call conventions and draw up new constitutions which would give blacks the vote and prevent former Confederate leaders from voting. If Congress approved the new constitution, and the state legislature ratified the Fourteenth Amendment, then the state would be readmitted. The southerners got around this act by not calling constitutional conventions. So Congress passed another Reconstruction Act requiring the military authorities who were occupying the states to register voters and supervise the election of delegates to constitutional conventions. Southerners defeated the new constitutions by not going to the polls, because the law stated that a majority of registered voters had to ratify the document.

1868, Reconstruction Act. A law stating that state constitutions were to be ratified by a majority of the voters, not a majority of those who had registered to vote.

Radical Republicans and Their Program

Charles Sumner (1811–1874). Leader of the ultra-Radical Republicans who insisted on immediate racial equality. He, along with Thaddeus Stevens, believed that the southerners had committed "state sui-

---

ANDREW JOHNSON (1808–1875), 17th President

Born in North Carolina and moved to Tennessee where he
  entered politics as a Jacksonian Democrat.
Member of the state legislature and of the House of
  Representatives.
Governor of Tennessee (1853–1857).
United States senator (1857–1862).
As a southerner loyal to the Union, he was appointed governor
  of federally occupied Tennessee in 1862.
Vice-president under Lincoln (March 4–April 15, 1865).
President (1865–1869).
Impeached by the House and came within one vote of conviction
  by the Senate in 1868.
Elected to the Senate in 1874 and died the next year.

---

cide" and should be treated during Reconstruction as conquered
provinces. Sumner was senator from Massachusetts from 1851 to 1874,
although he was absent for three years while recovering from the caning
administered by Representative Preston Brooks in 1856.

Thaddeus Stevens (1792–1868). A Radical Republican who supported Reconstruction policies which would protect the freedmen and
punish the Confederates, although he was willing to compromise to get
the votes of less radical Republicans. Stevens represented Pennsylvania
in the House as a Whig from 1848 to 1852 and as a Republican from
1859 to 1868. See his photograph on p. 459.

Benjamin Wade (1800–1878). Senator from Ohio who was a leader
of the Radical Republicans. During the Civil War he was chairman of
the Joint Committee on the Conduct of the War. See his picture on p.
459.

1865–1866, Black Codes. Laws passed in southern states to regulate the legal and employment status of the freed slaves. The codes
varied from state to state, and although some represented a considerable
improvement over slavery, others were designed to get around the Thirteenth Amendment and placed limitations on the freedom of former
slaves. Some codes recognized marriages and permitted blacks to sue
and testify in court and to own certain types of property. But some
states also passed codes stating that freed persons would not carry
weapons, take jobs other than farming and domestic work, or leave their
jobs without losing back pay.

1865–1872, Freedmen's Bureau. A branch of the War Department designed to coordinate efforts to help the freed slaves. Its most important function was helping them in the job market, defending their right to select their own employer, and to receive a just wage. The bureau also founded schools and provided food and medical care. Note the picture on p. 469.

1866, Civil Rights Act. A law which declared that blacks were citizens of the United States; the measure overturned the Dred Scott decision (1857) and was later confirmed by the Fourteenth Amendment (1868). The act also tried to negate some of the Black Codes by declaring that states could not restrict blacks' rights to testify in court and to hold property. President Johnson vetoed the bill, feeling that it violated states' rights, but Congress overrode his veto with a two-thirds majority in each House. The 1866 Civil Rights Act was the first major piece of legislation to become law over the veto of a president. Radical Republicans were afraid that it would be declared unconstitutional; so they initiated the Fourteenth Amendment.

1868, Fourteenth Amendment. An amendment passed by Congress in 1866 and ratified by three-fourths of the states in 1868 after the southern states had been instructed in the Reconstruction Act that they would not be readmitted to the Union until they did so. The amendment provided that: (1) all persons born or naturalized in the United States were citizens; (2) no state could "deprive any person of life, liberty, and property, without due process of law"; (3) southern states must grant blacks the vote or have their representation in Congress reduced; (4) former state or national officials who had joined the Confederacy could not hold another office unless specifically pardoned by a two-thirds vote of Congress; and (5) the Confederate war debt was not to be paid. The Fourteenth Amendment was an important milestone in centralizing political power at the national level, for it reduced the power of all the states.

1867, Tenure of Office Act. This prohibited the president from removing officials who had been appointed with the consent of the Senate without first getting the Senate's approval to dismiss them. President Johnson felt this act was unconstitutional and deliberately violated it by dismissing Secretary of War Edwin Stanton, who was in open sympathy with the Radical Republicans. This action gave the Radicals the excuse they had been looking for to impeach Johnson.

1868, Impeachment of Johnson. The president can only be removed from office after being impeached and convicted of "Treason, Bribery, or other high Crimes and Misdemeanors." Impeachment is accomplished by a majority vote in the House of Representatives, and conviction requires a two-thirds vote in the Senate, where the case is tried, presided over by the Chief Justice. Johnson was impeached, that is, charged, on 11 counts, most of them dealing with violation of the Tenure of Office Act. This largely political effort on the part of the Radical Republicans to get rid of Johnson was unsuccessful—barely. The Radicals failed by one vote to rally the two-thirds necessary for conviction. See Johnson's photograph on p. 458.

1870, Fifteenth Amendment. A constitutional change which guaranteed the vote to freed male slaves. It stated that the vote could not be denied "on account of race, color, or previous condition of servitude."

Politics and the Economy in the South

POLITICS

Black Republican governments. Governments in the southern states during Reconstruction in which blacks for the first time participated, generally voting Republican. Although blacks were elected to a number of political positions, the real rulers of the "black Republican governments" were white carpetbaggers and scalawags.

Carpetbaggers. Northerners who came South during Reconstruction and often took advantage of the black vote. They were a varied group: idealists eager to help the freedmen, employees of the federal government, and enterprising adventurers. Carpetbaggers got their name from the fact that they often arrived with their possessions in a carpetbag, an old-fashioned suitcase made out of material which looked like a carpet or rug.

Scalawags. White Republican southerners who during Reconstruction cooperated with the black out of a desire either to help him or to exploit his vote. Some were planters and merchants who had been Whigs, but most were people from areas that had had small slave populations and who had continued to support the Union during the war.

Union League of America. A club used by white southern Republicans to control the black vote. The organization employed secret rituals and symbols to appeal to blacks and get them to join. Then they had to swear to support the League list of candidates on election day.

Ku Klux Klan. An organization of white southerners which attempted to counteract the activities of the Union League and drive blacks out of politics. The name is based on the Greek word *kuklos,* which means "circle." The Klan was strongest from 1868 to 1872 and was a major force in destroying the Radical Republican governments in the South. The Ku Klux Klan, which is in existence today, is descended from a group which organized in 1915. The revived Klan is not only antiblack but also anti-Roman Catholic and anti-Jew.

1870–1871, Force Acts. Laws passed by Congress to protect black voters from the Klan. The acts placed elections under federal rather than local jurisdiction and imposed fines and prison sentences on persons convicted of interfering with a citizen's voting.

ECONOMY

Sharecropping. A system of cultivating the large plantations at a time when there was little cash to pay wages and the freedmen had no money to invest in land or tools. The plantation owner divided his land into small units, placing a black tenant on each one. In exchange for housing, tools, and other supplies, the black family provided labor. As rent, the sharecropper agreed to turn over a portion, or share, of his crop, usually 50 percent.

Crop-lien system. A method of financing agriculture when money was in short supply. Local merchants extended credit to planters for supplies in return for a lien, or mortgage, on the growing crop. At harvest time, the farmer turned over his crop to the merchant who marketed it and returned what was left after paying off the debt. Generally, the local storekeeper or banker would insist that a cash crop, such as cotton, tobacco, or sugar, be planted, thus contributing to a one-crop dependency rather than diversified farming. Note the graph "Southern Agriculture, 1850–1900" on p. 471.

ULYSSES SIMPSON GRANT (1822–1885), 18th President

Born in Ohio and graduated from West Point.
Served in the Mexican War.
Resigned from the army and shifted from job to job between 1854 and 1861.
Became the outstanding Union general in the Civil War and brought the war to conclusion at Appomattox.
President (1869–1877).

Elections

ELECTION OF 1872
Republican: Ulysses Grant
Liberal Republican: Horace Greeley

Democrat: Horace Greeley

Grant, the incumbent, received the Republican nomination. But a faction of the party, distressed by rumors of corruption and disappointed by Grant's failure to achieve civil service reform, set up their own party, the Liberal Republican. Their candidate was Horace Greeley, eccentric editor of the New York *Tribune*. The Democrats also nominated Greeley, but Grant carried the election.

ELECTION OF 1876

Republican: Rutherford Hayes

Democrat: Samuel Tilden

In this election the electoral votes of three states—Florida, South Carolina, and Louisiana—were in dispute, with both the Republicans and the Democrats claiming a majority in each of those states. Recall that the winner in each state receives all of that state's electoral votes. To decide who had won, a special Electoral Commission was established, not to be confused with the electoral college, which was to decide whether the Republican electoral votes or the Democratic electoral votes would be accepted from those states. The Commission was made up of five representatives, five senators, and five justices, with eight of them being Republicans and seven, Democrats. A vote of eight to seven decided that the Republicans had carried those states, and Hayes was elected president with an electoral vote of 185 to 184 for Tilden. The election is significant because it was settled by compromises rather than a return to the battlefield. See the map on p. 478.

Compromise of 1877. An informal agreement reached between Democrats and Republicans in which the Democrats consented not to contest the election if they were granted certain concessions. Hayes agreed to withdraw the last federal troops from the South, to appoint a southern ex-Whig to the Cabinet, and to push federal funding of internal improvement projects in the South. Thus a Republican became president, but with the troops gone, the South regained control of its political affairs, became solidly Democratic, and blacks increasingly lost the rights they had gained. Note the map "The South Returns to the Union" on p. 463.

OTHER TERMS TO IDENTIFY

John Wilkes Booth (1838–1865). An actor who shot President Lincoln in Ford's Theatre in Washington, D.C., on April 14, 1865. He and his co-conspirators felt they were avenging the South, not realizing that their hopes for a moderate peace lay in Lincoln. Booth was shot and killed two weeks later when forces surrounded and burned the barn where he was hiding at Bowling Green, Virginia.

Andersonville. The largest Confederate prisoner of war camp for Union soldiers, constructed in Georgia in 1864. In the summer of 1864 it contained 32,000 prisoners, and overcrowding and lack of medical facilities led to the spread of diseases from which almost one-half died. After the war the prison's Confederate commander, Captain Henry Wirz, was charged with murder, convicted, and hanged.

"Forty acres and a mule." A slogan widely popular among southern blacks in 1865. The idea was supported by Congressman Thaddeus Stevens who wanted to confiscate the property of leading Confederates and distribute it among the blacks. In reality, little land went into the hands of freedmen, who did not have the money to buy tools and seeds.

Whiskey Ring. A scandal during the Grant administration involving Grant's private secretary, Orville E. Babcock, who was in collusion with Treasury officials to help a group of St. Louis distillers avoid paying taxes on distilled whiskey. The fraud was eventually revealed, and 283 persons were indicted although most, including Babcock, escaped conviction.

Wormley Conference. A meeting between Republican and Democratic leaders on February 26, 1877, at the Wormley Hotel which led to Rutherford Hayes receiving the disputed electoral votes in exchange for certain concessions to the South.

GLOSSARY

antebellum. The term literally means "before the war." In the United States, it generally is used in reference to the pre-Civil War period.

façade. The face or front of a building or the portrayal of a fake or artificial front or image. When the Electoral Commission met to determine who should receive the votes in the 1876 election, the atmosphere of judicial inquiry and deliberation was a façade. The decision was really made along party lines.

franchise. A privilege or right granted to a person or group by the government, particularly the right to vote. Black males were given the franchise by the Fifteenth Amendment. The term now often refers to authorization by a manufacturer to a dealer to sell his products.

levee. An embankment raised to prevent a river from overflowing. During Reconstruction in the South, tax rates zoomed, but some of the proceeds were used to rebuild crumbling levees. The same word can also be used to refer to a very formal reception, such as President George Washington's inaugural levee in 1789.

maverick. An unbranded or orphaned calf or colt on the range. The term originated with Samuel Maverick (1803–1870), a Texas cattleman who did not brand his cows. The word also refers to someone, particularly in politics, who does not follow the group. Andrew Johnson was considered a maverick.

point of order. In parliamentary procedure, it is a question as to whether that which is being discussed is in order or allowed by the rules. If an individual wishes to raise

such a question, he says, "I rise to a point of order." Such parliamentary procedures were not always adequately understood by elected freedmen who used them
in the Black Republican governments.

Saint Sebastian.   A young Roman martyr of the 3rd century who was tied to a stake
and killed with arrows for having embraced Christianity. According to the New
York *Times* in 1877, Justice Joseph Bradley was criticized so vehemently by the
Democrats for having sided with Hayes rather than Tilden when the Electoral
Commission's vote was counted, that he seemed like "a middle-aged Saint Sebas-
tian stuck full of Democratic darts."

Solomon.   King of Israel in the 10th century B.C., who was particularly noted for his
wisdom. Even a Solomon would have been hard pressed to judge rightly as to
whether the Republicans or the Democrats had really won in 1876 in Florida,
South Carolina, and Louisiana.

Tweed Ring.   The corrupt political machine in New York City from around 1859 to
1871 which was notorious for its payoffs and kickbacks. William Marcy "Boss"
Tweed (1823–1878) was the political boss and was finally jailed for his activities.

"unredeemed" southern states.   The states which were still occupied by Union forces
and thus had not reconstituted their own state governments.

WORDS TO KNOW

Define the following, using the dictionary if necessary.

chicanery   obloquy
brigandage   pathological
diatribes   progeny
excoriating   recalcitrance

SAMPLE QUESTIONS

Matching

1. _____ The assassin of
President Lincoln in
1865.

2. _____ Commandant of
Andersonville military
prison and the only
southerner executed
for war crimes.

3. _____ The Radical
Republican from
Pennsylvania who
supported giving every

a. Samuel Tilden.
b. Rutherford Hayes.
c. Thaddeus Stevens.
d. Andrew Johnson.
e. Ulysses Grant.
f. Salmon Chase.
g. John Wilkes Booth.
h. Edwin Stanton.
i. Horace Greeley.
j. Henry Wirz.

adult male ex-slave
"forty acres and a
mule."

4. _____ The secretary of war
who was dismissed by
the president in
"violation" of the
Tenure of Office Act.

5. _____ The only president
who has been
impeached by a
majority vote in the
House of
Representatives.

6. _____ The chief justice who
presided at the trial in
the Senate after the
president had been
impeached.

7. _____ Republican president
who was personally
honest but whose
administrations were
notorious for scandal.

8. _____ New York *Tribune*
editor and unsuccessful
presidential candidate
of the Liberal
Republican and
Democratic parties.

9. _____ The former governor
of New York who lost
the presidential
election of 1876.

10. _____ As a result of the
Compromise of 1877,
this Republican
became president.

Multiple Choice

1. Which of the following was not a part of the Reconstruction program legislated by Congress?
   a. Black Codes.
   b. First Reconstruction Act.
   c. Freedmen's Bureau.
   d. Civil Rights Act.
2. The South developed an agricultural system in which the planter
   provided housing and agricultural supplies while families, usually
   black, provided labor. This system was called:
   a. sharecropping.
   b. gang labor.
   c. tenant farming.
   d. wage-crop economics.
3. The First Reconstruction Act of 1867:
   a. abolished the Ku Klux Klan.
   b. provided for military control of the South.
   c. left intact existing southern governments.
   d. was favored by President Johnson.
4. The Fourteenth Amendment did all except:
   a. give citizenship to the freedman.
   b. cancel Confederate war debts.
   c. free the slaves.
   d. guarantee payment of the Union war debt.
5. The Union League of America:
   a. kept the blacks from voting.
   b. worked to make the blacks loyal to the Republican party.
   c. provided food and clothing to the destitute in the South.
   d. elected Lincoln and Johnson in 1864.

ANSWERS
Matching: 1. g 2. j 3. c 4. h 5. d 6. f 7. e 8. i 9. a 10. b
Multiple Choice: c, d, b, c, b